CW01652840

SERVICE DESIGN FOR BUSINESS

SERVICE DESIGN FOR BUSINESS

A Practical Guide to Optimizing the Customer Experience

BEN REASON
LAVRANS LØVLIE
MELVIN BRAND FLU

WILEY

Service Design for Business:
A Practical Guide to Optimizing the Customer Experience

Authorised reprint by Wiley India Pvt. Ltd., 4435-36/7, Ansari Road, Daryaganj, New Delhi-110002.

Copyright © 2016 by Livework Studio Ltd. All rights reserved.

Published by John Wiley & Sons, Inc., Hoboken, New Jersey.

No part of this book, including interior design, cover design, and icons, may be reproduced or transmitted in any form except with the permission of John Wiley & Sons, Inc., 111 River Street, Hoboken, NJ 07030, (201) 748-6011, fax (201) 748-6008, or online at http://www.wiley.com/go/permissions.

Limit of Liability/ Disclaimer of Warranty: The publisher and the author make no representations or warranties with respect to the accuracy or completeness of the contents of this work and specifically disclaim all warranties, including without limitation warranties of fitness for a particular purpose. No warranty may be created or extended by sales or promotional materials. The advice and strategies contained herein may not be suitable for every situation. This work is sold with the understanding that the publisher is not engaged in rendering legal, accounting, or other professional services. If professional assistance is required, the services of a competent professional person should be sought. Neither the publisher nor the author shall be liable for damages arising herefrom. The fact that an organization or website is referred to in this work as a citation and/or a potential source of further information does not mean that the author or the publisher endorses the information the organization or website may provide or recommendations it may make. Further, readers should be aware that Internet websites listed in this work may have changed or disappeared between when this work was written and when it is read.

TRADEMARKS: Wiley, the Wiley logo are trademarks or registered trademarks of John Wiley & Sons, Inc. and/or its affiliates, in the United States and other countries, and may not be used without written permission. All other trademarks are the property of their respective owners. Wiley Publishing, Inc. is not associated with any product or vendor mentioned in this book.

Wiley also publishes its books in a variety of electronic formats. Some content that appears in print may not be available in electronic books.

This edition is authorized for sale in the Indian Sub-continent only.

Reprint: 2016

Printed at: Rakmo Press Pvt. Ltd., Delhi.

ISBN: 978-81-265-6006-6

Contents

For additional content on the topics discussed in this book, case studies and service design tools and approaches, visit: www.liveworkstudio.com/SDforB

Introduction

Design is trending in business. Business gurus are writing about design and the value it offers to more traditional business practice to enable innovation, collaboration, and creativity. Forrester Research describes service design as "the most important design discipline." Businesses like Apple, Dyson, and Philips have raised the awareness of the value of design to business. Other major businesses are bringing design capabilities in-house. IBM is building its Design Studio. Capital One Bank acquired leading design agency Adaptive Path. Mayo Clinic has its own design practice. The U.K. government is hiring designers in areas including tax and revenue and justice. Leading management consultancies are recognizing the value of design, too. McKinsey has bought design studio Lunar. Accenture acquired Fjord in the digital design space.

In light of these developments, we want to help business and government organizations understand what design can do for services—but what is service design? Service design is the design of services. When we started Livework in 2001, we wanted to have a positive impact on the way people live and work. Service design is helping us make that impact—it improves and innovates the services we use day to day. Banking and insurance, health care, transportation, business services, and a wealth of government activities are all services.

Organizations spend significant time designing tangible products. Services receive less design attention; however, to succeed in today's marketplace, this needs to change. Generally, services are less productive and cause more frustration to customers than products. We love our BMWs more than our banks. Service design addresses this quality and productivity gap.

Service design has been around for 20 years and has matured from a niche design discipline to a more comprehensive and accessible way to tackle customer, business, and organizational challenges. However, it is still under-recognized and undervalued by businesses. This book aims to address this in two ways: first, by putting the value of service design into business terms, and second, by showing how service design can connect to core business outcomes and capabilities.

Reading this book should give you a clear understanding of how you can use service design for specific challenges in your organization and what results to expect from doing so.

Who This Book Is For

This book is for people in businesses or large organizations. It aims to be valuable to those involved in business-to-consumer, business-to-business, and government services. As all services ultimately service human beings, there are common principles and tools that can be used across all sectors.

Service design can help start-ups, small and mid-sized enterprises (SMEs), and large organizations design better services. In this book, we focus mostly on challenges faced by many large or established organizations. Start-ups can use service design effectively, but we have focused on challenges that we see faced by our clients in large or established organizations. These are the challenges of change, collaboration, innovation, and customer focus that many big outfits face.

We identified three types of audience that we think will benefit from this book.

People Who Focus on Customers

Our first group is people who *care* about customers, or who are in a role where customers are a key consideration. You work in customer experience, insight, marketing, customer service, innovation management, or digital roles. Or you may be a leader who understands the importance of customers to your business and strategy.

Many people in these roles understand customers well and have insight into their experiences and needs. Often, though, you struggle to turn insight into action. You struggle to develop designs for improved customer experience, to generate concepts for how to compete for customers' attention and loyalty and to make these ideas tangible and realistic.

You may also struggle to connect customer insight to change in the organizations we work for. Great ideas fall on deaf ears and either fail to get support or get watered down in implementation when they encounter the challenge of changing the way a business operates. This can be due to the challenge of communicating to others, collaborating on a shared vision, or understanding the mechanisms that need to change.

For you, this book starts on familiar customer territory. It also gives you insight into how to better structure insight into service experiences in order to manage improvement and innovation through the business and organization.

People Who Are Focused on the Business

If you are in a strategic or commercial role, such as sales, retention, or growth, your focus is on performance and business results. However, understanding customers, their behaviors, choices, and needs are critical and have a big impact on performance.

In services, performance is dependent on customer behavior. Strategies flounder on the reality of the marketplace, and business models work in the abstract but do not always translate into results. Strategy needs to be more experimental to interface with the customer's world. Business objectives require successful engagement of customers to meet desired outcomes.

This book helps you discover levers that move customers in positive ways. It also offers new and more action-oriented service design tools for business people to develop, test, and implement strategies that are effective in the market.

People Who Are Focused on the Organization

Our third group is people who are more internally focused. You work in a part of the organization that maintains business as usual and also receives requests for change and improvement from the business. Working in IT, HR, or operations, you may feel that there is a lack of clarity and joined-up thinking. The silo factor, which most large organizations describe, is most keenly felt internally.

In these roles, you need to understand what the goals are so you can support them with the right solution in your area of expertise. You need to know what the other moving parts are in the business so you can integrate effectively, and you need to keep the business-as-usual lights on.

All parts of a business have one thing in common: the customer. This book helps you see the organization through the lens of the customer. It provides service design tools that can help internal teams take more control of the demands that are made of them—the tools can also help to connect to colleagues on the business side and manage prioritization and change.

How to Navigate This Book

We have structured this book around 12 challenges where we have seen service design have business impact. These challenges are grouped into three areas: "The Customer Story," focusing on service design impacting on customer experience, "Business Impact," diving into how service design can be used to address business challenges, and "Organizational Challenge," where we go deeper into how service design can be used to work with the people, structures, and systems of organizations to help move things forward.

Before we get into the challenges, we set the scene in two ways. First, by introducing the basics that cover the key trends that we see as the conditions we live and work in, which provide the context for the emergence and value of service design. Second, we cover some of the core concepts of service design that are useful to understand before tackling the challenges.

After the basics we go into some more detail on foundations. This is an overview of what we see as fundamental aspects of services and how we can understand them better in order to innovate and improve service by design.

Finally, we finish the book by unpacking some of the key tools we use in day-to-day practice with the aim of leaving you better equipped to start your service design journey.

SERVICE DESIGN FOR BUSINESS

Chapter 1

Why Service Design

Service design has emerged in the early twenty-first century for a number of reasons, some of which we introduce in a driving trends section below. Service design also has a heritage that gives it a background and inheritance. Some of this is from older design approaches designed for mass manufacturing or communications. The arts of industrial design and of branding have influenced the thinking and practice of service design. Another strong influence has been from service marketing, which is where the first service blueprints were developed.

These two elements together—the why and the what—should provide a clear view on why service design, why now, and how it is relevant to you as a manager, leader, or business.

THREE TRENDS THAT MAKE SERVICE DESIGN RELEVANT TODAY

It is not a coincidence that service design has emerged in the twenty-first century. Just as industrial and product design emerged with the development of mass manufacturing, service design is responding to some significant economic, social, and technical trends. Three trends, one in each of these categories, set the context for why service design is a growing discipline and of growing interest to more and more businesses and organizations.

Economic: The Trend Toward Value in Services

As economies mature, they move from agriculture to raw materials to manufacturing to services. This trend is a macro one and has already taken place in much of the world. Services comprise 70 to 80 percent of the economies of mature countries and are growing rapidly even in big producer countries such as Brazil. This trend should be thought of as less a replacement of the previous situation but a layering where services add value to manufacturers. Many industries are seeing services as higher-margin businesses than manufacturers.

As differentiation in products reduces with the maturity of industries, services prove to be the area where there is higher potential. Services have the additional benefit of supporting customers to get the best from products and drive loyalty. Service design was invented to respond to this trend, to bring the best design methodologies to bear on a new challenge. The achievement of design in manufacturers is well documented—in industries from automotive to electronics. Design needed to develop to offer these qualities to a new market.

Social: The Increase in Customer Expectations

Consumers are expecting more as they value their own entitlements more than previous generations. Where once people accepted what they got, market economies have trained individuals to expect more. This is accentuated when leading brands create excellent experiences that lead consumers to think, "Why can't all my experiences be like that?" Service providers that were one-size-fits-all, and you get what you are given, have to rethink their approach as customer expectations grow. Government services need to keep up, too, as politics drives them to improve customer experience through national surveys and directives.

This trend in consumer expectations bleeds into the business-to-business arena. Workers used to put up with experiences that were suboptimal and take the brunt of the pain with the logic that they could learn their way around and it was a part of the job. Now the example set by the best consumer services leads people to expect the same at work.

As expectations rise, the need to understand customer needs and expectations develops in parallel. Service design is one strong way to bring the new customer power into the design and improvement of services in a structured and productive manner.

Technical: Growth of Digital Means Change in Services

We are all aware of the impact of *the digital revolution*. It may be a cliché, but digital technologies have driven radical change and disruption in the service sector. Services that were previously delivered by humans who had a level of expertise can now be partially delivered by technology. Think of financial advice or banking that used to be face-to-face but is more and more online and self-serve. Digital has impacted almost every service sector. Digital disrupts in other ways, too. It can change the established dynamics of a sector and enable new entrants to markets. Amazon in retail is the most obvious example.

The potential for change in service, and the fact that what were primarily human-delivered service are now mediated by technology, has driven the need for service design. Technology can dehumanize and make things harder to navigate for customers and less flexible. Service design offers tools to domesticate and humanize technology.

USE SERVICE DESIGN TO DEAL WITH BUSINESS AMBITIONS AND ORGANIZATIONAL CHALLENGES

Connecting Customers to the Business and the Organization

Service design offers a perspective, method, and tool set that enables an organization to realize business ambitions as well as a way to deal with internal and external challenges. It offers an approach to deal with strategic initiatives as well as operational challenges by asking three fundamental questions:

1. What does this do for our current and future customers?
2. How will our business be impacted?
3. Which capabilities are needed by the organization to respond or to drive the initiative?

The main objective of the approach is to resolve customer-related challenges, but balance them with business drivers and the organizations' capabilities. Other times, understanding the customers' perspective will provide clarity and direction needed to achieve business results or to drive organizational change. It is important to separate business concerns from the people, structures, and capabilities that make up the organization. In all cases, service design starts by taking an outside-in perspective, and drive this through real business objectives while considering an organization's capabilities.

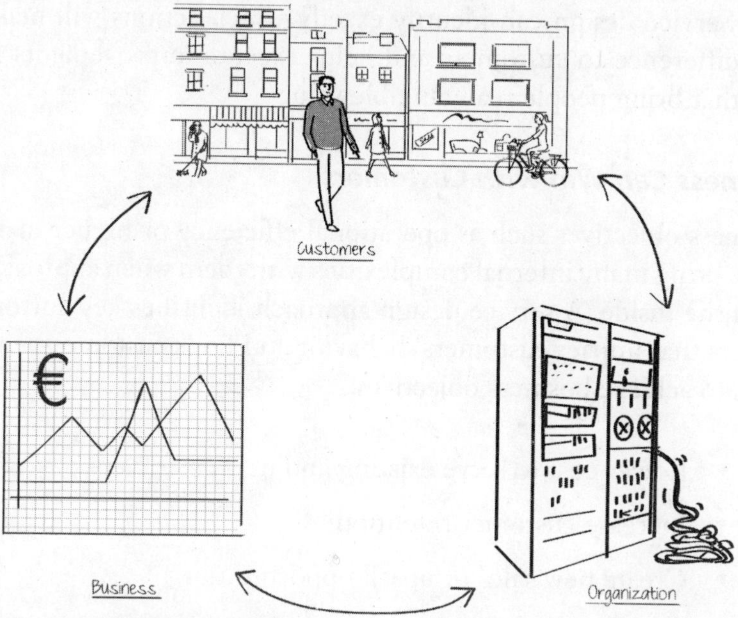

Customer-Business-Organization

Understand Customers and Build High-Value Relationships

Seeing a business through customers' eyes offers powerful insights that make customers' expectations, experience, and behavior more tangible. It exposes customers' pain points and provides deeper understanding of their emotions as they interact and transact with a business. This enables companies to identify clear intervention points that can be leveraged to increase value for customers and deal with challenges, typically to:

- Increase customer satisfaction and improve the level of adoption
- Reduce customer irritations and prevent costly service failures
- Improve service experience for customers and build better customer relations

Service design can identify exactly which actions will make a real difference to customers and helps execute improvements in a way that bring people real, tangible value.

Business Can Win with Customers

Business objectives such as operational efficiency or higher market share bring many internal complexities with them when approached from the inside. A service design approach identifies key customer drivers that impact customers' behavior and finds customer-centric ways to achieve business objectives:

- Lower cost to serve existing and new customers.
- Increase customer retention.
- Create new sales or upsell opportunities.
- Successfully launch product and service innovations into the market.

Solutions to business challenges can be surprisingly simple when taking an outside-in approach to expose what is really relevant to customers and when used to find solutions in other sectors and businesses. A service design approach can help both to imagine radical solutions to complex problems and to implement many small incremental improvements that together create massive top-line and bottom-line impact.

Align the Organization around Customers

Aligning departments, channels, partners, and stakeholders requires management focus, as does the need to optimize and adjust the internal workings of the organization. This creates a strong internal focus in many organizations lose sight of the fact that the most important customer is the external customer which results in practices, systems, and processes that do not serve customers, or worse, create obstacles for staff and customers. Understanding customers—especially their needs and expectations of the organization—translated to the reality of how the organization operates and runs enables organizations to achieve:

- Internal understanding and alignment
- High staff engagement and participation
- More customer-centric focus, leading to increased market agility

A service design approach provides the customer as an outside reference not only to align people in an organization but also to deal with internal challenges around systems, processes, procedures, and policies.

The concept of service design as a way to approach customers, the business, and organization is a model we refer to in many of the chapters in this book as we go about explaining *how*.

KEY CONCEPTS

There are some key concepts that lie at the heart of service design, and understanding them helps you get the most out of this book. In this section, we explain concepts such as design thinking, qualitative customer research, and visualization and how they form a base for the service design approach to business.

The Design Approach

Companies often struggle to solve problems with the usual analytical and deductive tools. The design process offers a powerful alternative, providing a generative and creative approach to finding solutions.

Thinking By Doing

In business thinking, the assumption is that the answers to most problems are already out there. It is a matter of finding and evaluating different solutions, and then to selecting the right one for the particular market.

Design thinkers start from the assumption that there is a perfect solution out there, but it hasn't been invented yet. The design thinking approach helps you to imagine and test and redesign a solution quickly, until it matches the reality of the market. In practice, service design combines analytical and imaginative thinking.

Human-Oriented

Another fundamental starting point in design is empathy with the human (customer) and their experiences. When a business challenge involves being successful with customers, or inspiring staff to adopt new processes or ways of working, this is a great advantage. Seeing the business through your customers' eyes can help people from the CEO to operational teams to make better decisions.

Creative Processes

Design as an approach brings a whole raft of visual and creative methods to solve business challenges. Over the past two decades design thinking has shown that design processes can be applied not only to chairs and cell phones but also to complex problems like planning international security operations, optimizing hospital processes, and innovating banking services.

Creative design processes can seem both frivolous and confusing at first, but prove to have massive impact on bringing innovative services to market and bringing the organization along on challenging change journeys.

Qualitative Research

The service design approach puts emphasis on complementing quantitative research with qualitative methods. This enables teams to combine strong subjective understanding of the human experience with predictable patterns that apply to most customers. The result is services that not only satisfy customer needs and wants but also delight, inspire, and empower.

Insight versus Numbers

Market research is typically quantitative, based on large numbers of respondents, and delivers a few statistical "truths." Qualitative customer research can yield significant insight with a small number of respondents. Combining market facts with inspiring insights about the humans who actually buy your service increases your chances at achieving success in the market.

Understand Behavior

Qualitative research helps to uncover the aspects of human behavior that can't be seen in the numbers. Diving deep into a few customers' lives will reveal the motivations for their actions and expose other things they do that can't be explained in a questionnaire.

Observed customer behavior is a highly valuable source of information as it provides a clear picture of how customers really experience services in their everyday lives as well as their needs and values. This insight is useful in the creative process of developing services that work for customers.

When behavioral insight is combined with economics, the results can gain highly strategic impact.

Insights That Drive Success in Practice

Experiences are human and subjective and can't be quantified. This doesn't mean that customer experiences can't be approached in a rational way. A service design approach enables you to generate non-quantifiable insight with the same structure and rigor that applies to other research and development techniques.

Ultimately, knowing your customers *as humans* makes it easier to shape every bit of service delivery to meet their needs and expectations—and design the interactions that delight and create desire.

The Power of Visual Storytelling

Visualization can be a powerful tool to take an organization from insight to results. It's particularly useful to better understand systems, processes, and customer experiences. Simple sketches and drawings can help clarify ideas, aid communications, and support convincing superiors, peers, and implementation teams.

Understand Complex Situations

Service delivery in today's marketplace often requires a complex integration of in-house and external IT systems. It involves multiple business functions and depends on a variety of processes to be well coordinated.

Visualization allows you to map these complex situations and creates an overview of all the parts and relationships between them. Maps, diagrams, and system drawings enable teams to *understand* situations better, gain a shared focus, and bring clarity to confusing information.

Communicate Ideas

Visualization helps people think and communicate. In the information-rich environments of business, access to knowledge is rarely the main challenge. What consumes time, effort, and brainpower is making ideas simple and understandable.

Drawings and designs are quick and effective ways to represent abstract ideas and can become highly potent tools for anyone who picks up a pen and stack of Post-its.

Describe Customer Experiences

One of our great role models, IDEO co-founder Bill Moggridge, wisely said, "You can't have an experience without experiencing it." Meaning that when you develop customer experiences that are made up by how people sense colors, space, shapes, and interactions, words lack the means to describe a target experience accurately.

Visualization of customer scenarios, retail spaces, websites, and cell phone interfaces and advertisements in the early strategic phases of development help you specify and communicate the target customer experience in much more precise ways. This helps you gain precision around business objectives and helps to identify how you reach them in practice.

Designing with People, Not for Them

Co-creation, often mentioned in conjunction with service design, is an approach to actively involve customers and staff in the creative aspects of developing services.

More traditional design approaches founded in product-centric companies focus on determining needs as a starting point for the development process, and then engineers develop the product before they are tested with customers before launch. This is an obvious way to go about development when the organization moves in product cycles of 6, 12, and 24 months.

In the service sector, things are different. Services are re-designed, optimized, and improved on a daily basis, while the service is up and running and being delivered by staff and experienced by customers. In this situation, it pays off to continually involve customers in the process of imagining new solutions and getting them ready for market.

Pull Ideas, Don't Push Them

An approach to designing with people recognizes that customers have clear needs and often good ideas about how they can be met. Opening up channels for customers to engage with development teams in creative ways, makes it easier to generate ideas that meet actual demands and desires. It's also a cheap and quick way to innovate

Design Solutions with Customers

Service excellence is primarily about continual improvement. Businesses that win are experts at avoiding customer irritations and inefficient delivery.

Actively allowing customers to contribute design ideas and combining this with observing their actual behavior provides a powerful basis to improve, design, and deliver experiences that really make a difference.

Design Solutions with Staff

The true service experts are the people that deliver the service every day. Some might meet customers face-to-face in a store, while others work behind the scenes in a logistics department.

In both cases, service employees have extremely detailed knowledge about what creates value for customers and what works for the business. Involving customer-facing staff in creative design helps decrease your chances of failure. The significant by-product is highly engaged staff that will embrace the improvement and change they were part of creating.

The Service Blueprint as Framework

When organizations struggle to satisfy their customers, they need to analyze the experience they deliver, understand when and how it adds value, and identify opportunities to improve the experience. The service blueprint can help do this: it gives a visual overview of all bits that constitute a service. The blueprint helps people in different areas of the organization see their part of the whole and resolves service delivery issues in a customer-oriented manner.

Align the Service to the Customer Journey

The service blueprint takes the customer journey as a starting point. It describes the service from the customer's point of view *before*, *during*, and *after* engagement. This outside-in view helps spot gaps and irritations in the interactions between the customer and the organization, as well as in the overall delivery of the service.

Front-Stage Channels and Back-Stage Processes

The service blueprint highlights how different front-stage channels such as web, face-to-face, call centers, smartphones, and even third-party services align to the customer journey. By mapping what each channel offers customers in their interactions with the organization, you quickly get an overview of how teams within the organization need to align their back-stage processes to meet customer expectations. This approach also helps to spot and visualize redundant and overlapping capabilities across channels and simplify service delivery.

Make Decisions with a Shared Overview

The service blueprint is a tool that enables people to gain a bird's-eye view of how the different elements of service align to create value for customers. This helps you make small and large decisions about actions you can take to make the service experience better for customers and more efficient for the business.

Service Blueprint

Chapter 2

Foundations

Three Critical Factors in Service Design

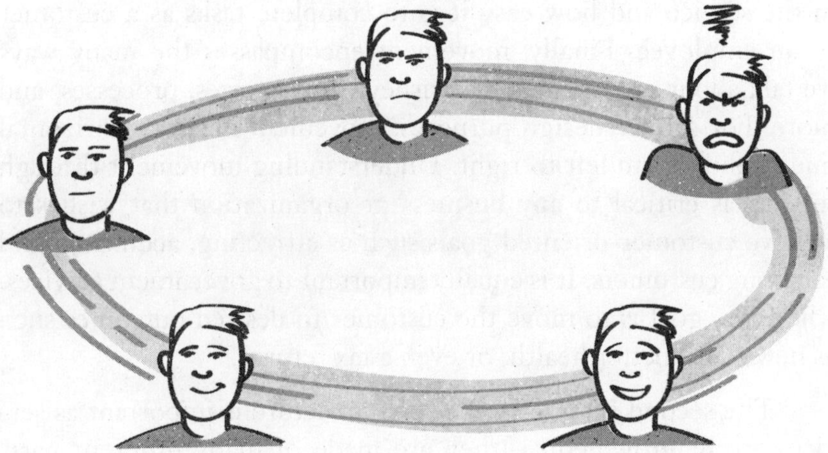

One of the challenges we face in focusing on services rather than products is that we do not have the same level of formal language to talk about services. Our industrial heritage and mind-set means that mechanical language is often used in what is a post-mechanical economy. In extreme cases service sector businesses like banks, utilities, and telecoms use industrial language to describe their operations. Some even have departments called *manufacturing*.

This section of the book aims to provide some formal language to use when discussing the creation and management of services. We focus on three key areas that are critical and introduce some terms within each area to help the discussion and description of services.

The first section is called *movement*. Movement is particular to services and is essential to understand to design and manage services. Movement means the movement through a service. This could be the movement of a customer on the journey from first awareness of the service offer through buying to using and one day maybe leaving the service. Movement can also be the movement of customers because services often have thousands of customers, and the management of these numbers is a critical factor in managing demand at different times. Movement is also a quality that is important in services. This quality is about how well things flow in the service and how easy it is to complete tasks as a customer or an employee. Finally, movement encompasses the many ways we talk about experiences, as journeys, user stories, processes, and more. For service design purposes, movement is also a horizontal line reading from left to right. Understanding movement through services is critical to any business or organization that wishes to achieve customer-oriented goals such as attracting, acquiring, and retaining customers. It is equally important to government services, where the goal is to move the customer to desired outcomes such as new skills, better health, or even a tax return.

The second section is *structure*. Structure is important as services are heterogeneous—they are made of many different parts brought together. For example, a bus service is a mix of vehicles, drivers, timetables, prices, and many more. Unlike the components of a product, these elements are not all present all of the time—they come and go at different points in services delivery. Structure can be the use of multiple channels to deliver a service. Understanding how we plan to use channels is the basis of customer engagement strategies. It can be the structure of an organization in terms of teams, departments, or functions or it can be the structure of measurements such as business performance. We use structure to categorize different aspects of a service and break what is a complex mix into manageable elements that we can look at separately and importantly, together in parallel. Structure contains the different ways we view a service, as an experience, an engagement, an organization, or as a performance. Structures can be mapped to movement as the vertical elements that are aligned to the horizontal movement. Understanding structures in services is valuable to be able to better organize yourselves in ways that deliver in a joined-up manner and get the best of the people and technologies at your disposal.

Finally, we have *behavior*. Behavior is what happens at the intersection of movement and structure. How do customers behave in different channels and when they shift channels? How do they behave in different situations or at different stages of their lives? How do people behave within the organization when they interact with customers or between each other? How do technologies behave? By placing behaviors within a framework of movement and structure, we can better understand current behaviors—of customers, staff, or technologies—and we can design for new behaviors, too. Once we can influence behaviors through design we can really start to impact business performance.

MOVEMENT

Alongside structure, movement is the critical quality of a service. Customers must move through phases and stages of a service relationship to get the service and to get the value from it. The language used in service design and other customer-oriented disciplines refers to movement in a number of ways, the most

Movement

common being customer journeys. This recognizes that there is a time-based dynamic to a service.

Service design helps to understand and design for this movement and to make it smoother, more successful, ultimately to enable customers to achieve their goals. Movement is represented as a horizontal in a lot of service design approaches—and we do this throughout this book. This helps to see the movement from left to right, but it is important to recognize that ultimately services are cyclical and there is movement from end to beginning, and within that there can be cycles within the larger journey.

Like Stories, Services Have a Before, Beginning, During, and After

> Telling stories about your customers' current and future experiences can lead to greater customer insight and better service designs.

Like any good tale, a narrative structure is comprised of four acts: before, beginning, during, and after. Understanding these acts in any customer experience will help to design better experiences and services.

Many organizations struggle to see the full picture from the customer's perspective and instead focus on a single aspect of the experience that is of importance to them. This may be the moment of sale or a moment of high importance to the organization, or it might be a performance such as a surgery or the delivery of a new car. How can organizations see the bigger picture—the one that comprises all aspects of the experience: before, beginning, during, and after? What happened to the customer before that could have a bearing on the sale? What happens to the customer after the moment of high importance? These questions can be key to the success of the service for both customers and the organization or business.

Stories about key life stages such as moving home or retiring can help to understand human needs in the customer lifecycle.

Before, Begin etc: *A simple framework that can provide the basic structure for understanding service experience from the customer perspective.*

Stories about customers' day-to-day experiences tell us about how they feel about a service and what stories they tell to others.

Let's investigate the four aspects of storytelling in service design a little deeper.

Before: Where Do Customers Come From?

It is important to know where your customers come from, what experiences they had prior to their engagement with your service, and what prejudices, expectations, and knowledge they bring with them. They have likely had experiences with competitors or other businesses similar to yours that color their expectations. For instance, in a sector like health care, they may have had previous attempts to address their health issues that affect their levels of understanding or trust.

Considering customers' experiences before their interactions with your organization gives you insight into the baggage they carry and better prepares your organization to respond to new customers' expectations.

Understanding what customers have experienced before they interact with your business can have a huge impact on sales and marketing strategies and approaches. This knowledge enables you to tailor sales approaches to meet a customer's need for reassurance or information. It can also enable you to market and communicate in ways that address specific perceptions and develop propositions that meet unmet needs or differentiate your services in the market.

For some government services, it is common for customers to move from one service to another—from police to judicial, for example. Customers often fall through the gaps after one service and before the next. In these cases, understanding customers' situations *before* they use a specific service can greatly impact the integration of services and overall customer outcomes.

Beginning: The Start of Your Relationship

How customers begin their relationship with a service is critical to success. It significantly impacts retention and the cost to serve customers later in life. A good beginning helps to avoid dissatisfaction and makes customers more disposed to do more business with you later.

In a broader context, "beginnings" can refer to the importance of how customers experience the start of new phases of their lives. How people embark on education, parenthood, or begin to live with a health condition is critical to their later success. These new beginnings are often also the start of a new service that must support these good beginnings and enable better overall outcomes. Take an extreme example. A child starting a new school is the beginning of a service. Good schools put care and attention into ensuring a good start, as they know that settled happy children will learn more effectively.

The same is true for how customers begin more day-to-day experiences such as signing a contract (a new phone tariff or an insurance premium) or life with a new product (especially complex ones like a car or a boiler). The beginning, in more technical terms the setup, establishes the value the customer gets from the service or product and therefore how they perceive your business and the value they have received—which is often different from the value you may think you have delivered. Think of the negative impact of a customer starting a new contract already feeling that things are not quite right, and check to make sure you are delivering what you think you are.

During: Day-to-Day Experience and Special Events

In storytelling terms the during part is where there are ups and downs, things work out but then a problem occurs, or something catastrophic happens and must be resolved. This part of a story varies depending on the type of story. The same is true for services. Some are constantly dealing with emergencies—like a fire service or emergency hospital—others carry on fairly smoothly with the odd little niggle or event—like a school or a train service.

These ups and downs in services are the planned and the unplanned aspects of customers' experiences. Planned is what customers expect to get because it is part of the contract, for example, to be able to make regular calls and text messages. Unplanned is what they expect help with when things don't go according to plan—replace my dropped or stolen phone.

There are a number of reasons why it's critical to continue to think about the customer's experience, or story, during their use of a service. The first is that businesses often "switch off" once customers purchase or sign up, and promptly neglect them—which leaves them to feel uncared for. Customer service is often thought of as a cost and something most businesses would rather not bother with. This leads to customer dissatisfaction and defection.

The second reason is that customers change. During the life of their contract or relationship with your organization, changes in their situation may affect their needs—and unless you are able to respond to these shifting needs, your value to the customer will diminish. A simple change like moving can hugely impact the customer's experience of your service. Designing how you support these changes during the experience helps to stay relevant and valued by customer, as with a home move, which is always an opportunity to help customers.

Finally, there are always unplanned aspects of our experiences of services where things do not go smoothly. Perhaps there is a delay or a fault in service delivery and the customer needs it to be fixed.

Unless businesses respond well to these events, you will become worse in customers' eyes. Incidents may be simple or complex, but if the customer notices them, then they are important to them and therefore have a heightened impact on their opinion of a service.

After: What Do Customers Do Next?

Past customers are also potential future customers—and are therefore always worth attention. It is surprising how many organizations fail to consider the experience of customers after they have used their services. Some switch to another brand but could come back, especially if they are welcomed as former customers.

For example, in government services, customers who leave a service could well bring new demands on a following service. This happened in the United Kingdom where lower levels of service in hospitals led to greater demand for community health care. If they are not supported after their use, there is a possibility that they will relapse or encounter a new avoidable crisis.

Paying attention to customers after they use your services can mean keeping in touch with them or simply ensuring that the service they have transitioned to is prepared to meet their needs. Because the "after" of one service is the "beginning" of another.

Finally, customers reflect on their experiences. Even if customers you contact after they have left do not renew their business with you, the information you can gather about their reasons for leaving can help prevent future losses. These insights are valuable.

Takeaway Messages

1. Customers' experience begins before they engage with your organization.
2. The beginning sets the tone for the relationship.
3. Customers' needs can change during their relationship.
4. Past customers can be future customers, too.
5. One service's former customers are another's future customers.

Designing Customer Journeys in the Context of Lifecycles

> Customer lifecycles and customer journeys enable you to understand what customers experience and help you design improvements to these experiences.

Customer Lifecycles

Customer lifecycles are frameworks to help us understand how the majority of customers experience a service. The customer lifecycle describes the relationship between an organization and its customers. This enables us to view a service or a whole sector through the customers' eyes. Lifecycles are phase-by-phase descriptions of how customers move from initially becoming aware of a service to becoming a customer who uses a services and eventually either renewing or leaving.

Lifecycles help us see things the customers do on their own that are critical to service success, such as choosing a service or changing their needs during the use of a service—aspects of the experience

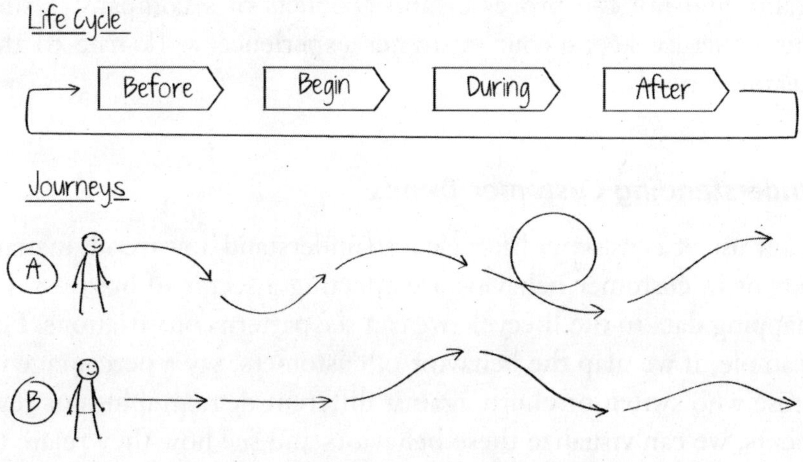

Lifecycles and journeys: *Where a lifecycle provides structure, journeys describe different experiences within the overall framework.*

that organizations frequently miss. Customer lifecycles also help us structure our analysis of customer experience and behaviors and to identify where a service is failing or can be improved.

The power of customer lifecycles appears in a detailed understanding of what influences customers' behavior and decisions. Customer lifecycles enable a clear view of behaviors and experiences that apply to a significant number of customers. This provides businesses with powerful strategies for engaging with customers better.

Using a customer lifecycle provides a baseline framework for customer experience at a strategic level in a number of ways.

Maintaining an Outside-In Perspective

A customer lifecycle is a description of phases and stages that customers go through when engaging with services in a specific sector. It is not unique to one business or brand. The lifecycle of insurance, public transport, or equipment maintenance is common to competitors or parallel providers in a sector. Customers buying insurance coverage have the same needs independent of provider. This is important as it is how the lifecycle reflects the outside customer reality and not the processes and products of a company. Using this structure keeps your customer experience work true to the customer needs.

Understanding Customer Trends

A key use of a customer lifecycle is to understand how trends in markets or in customer behavior are affecting a sector of business. By mapping data to the lifecycle we can see patterns or variations. For example, if we map the behavior of customers, say a percentage of those who switch or churn against different demographics or segments, we can visualize these behaviors and see how they relate to customer value or numbers. In this way lifecycles show key business factors in customer behavior terms.

Identifying Hotspots to Enable Strategic Focus

Lifecycles also enable more surgical analysis. For example, mapping customer complaints or fail points to the lifecycle can enable the discovery of key *hotspots* in the lifecycle where customer-related problems are taking place. This analysis can be done using existing customer data—complaints, satisfaction, and so on—or by designing data capture to pinpoint issues. Knowing where fail points are hitting large numbers of customers and are hampering business performance or causing unnecessary costs is invaluable in prioritizing actions.

Using Lifecycles to Understand a Range of Actors

It is easy for us to use consumer examples, but in a business-to-business setting the customer is more than one person. A typical business will have decision makers, financial controllers, managers, and end users all involved in using a product or service. For ease we call these different people 'actors'. Lifecycles can help us to understand how these different actors in an organization experience a service. We can then design services that will engage different actors in the right ways at the right times. This is not only useful for a business customer, it can also apply to families and to complex situations where a service may have multiple people in different roles—or actors—from different organizations who are using a service together—such as a courtroom or a school. The lifecycle is used as a common frame for all these actors, as they are all moving through the cycle in parallel. By identifying the roles each actor plays at each stage of the lifecycle, we can better understand their collective needs and behaviors.

Customer Journeys

Customer journeys describe how to deliver the right experience to each individual customer. Journeys provide step-by-step descriptions of a customer's path as he or she interacts with the organization. They visualize how a customer might engage through a range of channels from the web to a retail environment or a call center. Journeys describe the experience through each interaction.

Customer journeys are well-known customer experiences or service design tools—and understanding of their use and value is critical to their success.

A customer journey creates value when it helps an organization design how it should engage customers to create better performing services. It can effectively guide the organization's choices, investments, and activities and is therefore a critical tool.

Customer experiences are highly influenced by structural facts of a particular sector; therefore, it is important to be precise about how customer journeys interact with specific aspects of a business—as well as the sector it operates in. For example, all customers' experiences of telecom services are influenced by the technical fact that it is essential to create a network connection to the customer's device or home. These facts are the fundamentals of sector specific customer lifecycles. Because customer journeys take place within the context of a lifecycle, the journey can differ but the lifecycle remains steady. Using the telecom example, customers must move through the network setup phase of the service experience to receive their connection. However, the journey they take to get the setup completed can vary depending on how they interact with the service provider, through which channels and over what time period. Customer journeys enable us to explore the different ways that customers experience a service and to develop improved journeys that benefit customers and businesses.

Thinking of customer journeys as variable experiences through the more structured lifecycles of industries or services is particularly useful in regard to a number of important considerations covered below.

Customer Choice, Behavior, and Preference

Different customer types have different preferences, make different choices, and behave in different ways. Designing journeys that describe how different customer types experience services can help to ensure that services are effective for many customers and enable specific customer groups to use a service in a way that suits them. This may mean enabling customers to move through a service at different speeds to avoid frustrating the speedy or rushing the deliberate. Sometimes it is useful to design journeys for both regular and new customers through the same processes. Alternatively, we may want to restrict customer choice but doing so deliberately and with due consideration of the impacts. In all these cases customer journeys enable you to prepare for a range of external customer factors.

Designing Journeys across Channels

Customer journeys help to get the most from the channels your organization uses to engage customers. Channels are often seen in isolation, but the best services enable customers to cross channels and guide customers to use the channels that are most effective. Journeys help us to describe how customers can move between channels, ensuring that each channel is able to pick up where the last left off. In cases where a business aims to migrate customers to a new channel, journeys help to design journeys that guide customers onto the new channel rather than simply switching the old one off or frustrating them by reducing its capacity to support them. For example, a technician who helps resolve a customer issue can then set up the customer with an online service channel to save them from waiting on the telephone for a response.

Takeaway Messages

1. Lifecycles provide understanding, journey helps us act.
2. Customer journeys can ensure flexibility.
3. Journeys can enable us to design for different customer types.
4. Journeys describe how channels work together.
5. Journeys describe how different people/actors experience a service between them.

Meeting Customer Needs and Expectations with Information, Interactions, and Transactions

Knowing what your customers need and expect at each point of their experience enables you to design more efficient and effective services.

Customers use services to fulfill a perceived need. Some needs are straightforward, such as the need to eat, travel, or find somewhere to stay on a trip. Others are complex and may not even be fully understood by the customer, such as the need for education or treatment for an illness. These needs are fairly steady and do not change hugely over time. In this way, needs are embedded in the service lifecycle as key elements that enable the successful performance of a service.

In addition to needs, customers have expectations of the services they use. Expectations are set by the market and by customers' prior experiences and pertain to customers' judgment of the quality of a service. A service may have delivered a specific outcome, getting the customers from A to B, but the manner of the service performance may not have met their expectations. And while they may not get their money back, they probably will not use the service again. Customers have expectations of how they will experience their needs being met, how they get the information, and how they interact and transact.

In simple terms, needs are for the *what* of the service, expectations are *how* it is delivered. The *what* is the substance of the service, the elements that can be specified in a contract or agreement. The *how* is the way it is delivered, the qualities and communications.

To provide some structure to this, we can break customer needs into three categories to enable us to be more specific in defining a need and also to help us think about the mechanisms we may use to meet that need. These categories are *information*, the need to know about someone or something, *interaction*, the need to engage

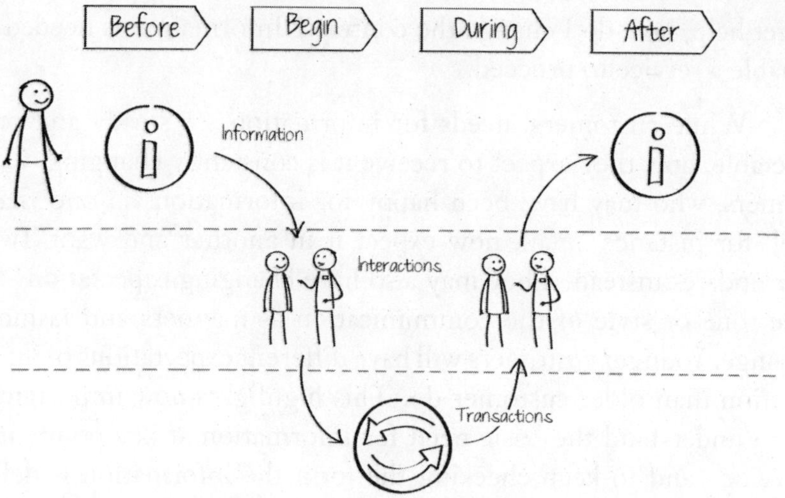

Information, interactions, and transactions: *These categories provide a way to break down a service into different aspects that customers need at different points in their experience. Customer journeys can be described to show how customers move between these three categories.*

with someone or something, and *transaction*, the need to make an exchange with someone or something.

Information

Customers need information to be empowered by a service. They need to be empowered to make decisions, to trust service providers, and to have the peace of mind that things are okay. Communication on information is often an issue for customers who are generally less well informed about important things like costs, timings, and performance than the service operator.

A common example is customers' need for information to make purchasing decisions. This can be critical to a service's performance: if customers cannot decide, they will not buy. Think about the difficulties faced making a range of decisions from purchasing travel tickets to phone tariffs to medical treatments. Customers also need information when they set up a service: How does it work, how do

I get help, how do I change the contract? Information is needed to enable a service to proceed.

While customers' needs for information are steady and predictable, how they expect to receive it is constantly changing. Customers, who may have been happy for information via one channel, for instance email, now expect it in another and want Twitter updates instead. They may also have changing expectations for the tone or style of the communication as manners and fashions change. Younger customers will have different expectations of information than older customer do. This highlights how important it is to understand the basic need for information at key points in a service—and to keep checking the form the information is delivered in.

Interactions

Information is not always enough to meet customers' needs. At times they will need to interact with a service in a way that enables the two parties to create something that moves the service forward. Customers need to interact with service providers in order to state their preferences or specific conditions that must be understood by the service. This could be dietary requirements, a legal situation, or medical history, among many examples.

Interactions are required at the points where the service becomes personal to the customer—where they need to tailor the service to their needs. This could be as simple as stating the time you would like to travel or as complex as the interactions between a student and teacher required for a teacher to deliver learning in a style that suits the individual.

Both simple and complex interactions enable service providers to build a relationship with customers. It may be a relationship captured in a customer relationship management (CRM) system or in the memory of the teacher—but it compels the service provider to be more accurate in their delivery and the customer's specific needs.

As with information, customers' expectations of interactions vary. Some may expect to interact in different channels dependent on their preferences; for example, preferring to bank at a branch or online. The style of the interaction is also important, in fact even more so, as customers will have expectations about how they are treated.

Customers expect certain levels of respect, attention, speed, and other qualities. As with all relationships, the quality of the interactions is significant to how we feel about the other party.

Transactions

Unlike other relationships, services always have a transactional element. Think of transactions as the contractual heart of the service. Customers need to transact with services at vital points—at the initial purchase or decision, at setup, at times when they need to change the contract, and when they renew or cancel. This may seem obvious, but service providers often make it so hard to transact that they lose customers.

Think of the contract that is so long you run out of patience, the ticket too complex to buy, or the provider who makes it so hard to change your contract that you find it easier to go elsewhere. Rules, regulations, and policies that the customer doesn't care about can over complicate transactions. This gets in the way of the customer's ability to transact with a service. Understanding what is essential to customers to complete the transaction rather than focusing on what you require will enable you to radically simplify the experience for the customers by meeting their needs—not the needs of the organization or the regulator.

While the kind of transactions customers need to make is steady, the trend is for customers to expect transactions to get easier and easier. This is driven by the best practice in some sectors and the fact that customers think that if one business can do it then why not your business. Customers expect growing levels of flexibility in their transactions and resent being fixed in unchangeable contracts.

Focusing on customer needs from transactions can improve their experience and also reduce your cost to serve.

Takeaway Messages

1. Customer needs are the what of services—the components.
2. Customer expectations are the how of services—the qualities.
3. Information supports decision making and trust.
4. Interactions enable a service to be personalized.
5. Transactions are both critical and overemphasized.

STRUCTURES

To design services, we need to understand the structures that define them. We may need to understand the existing structure of a service we wish to improve or the potential structure of a new service. The structure of a service includes the channels employed, the business architecture that the service is built upon, or the organizational structure that delivers the service.

A service design approach will define these structures and visualize them as parallel rows in a service blueprint or customer jour-

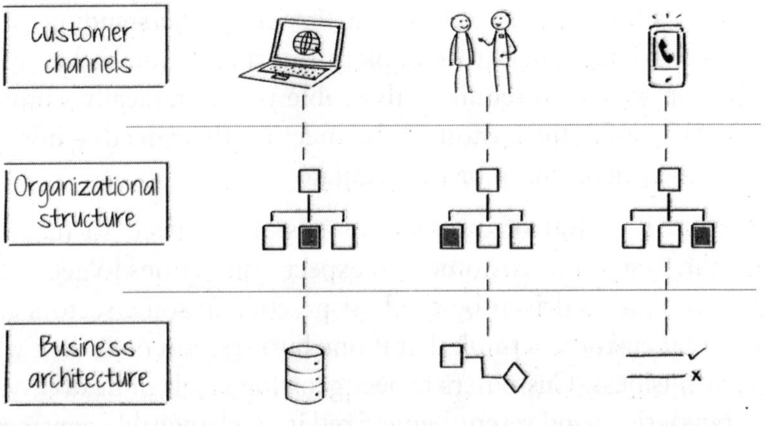

Structure

ney map. This enables us to see what part of the structure is involved when and what it is doing.

Human, Consumer, Customer, and User Lifecycles

Lifecycles help you understand how people behave in different roles, as humans, consumers, customers, and users.

Lifecycles represent an outside-in perspective of what customers experience across an industry sector. Unique characteristics exist for different industries and markets, but because humans tend to have several common behavior patterns, we can generalize some stages—like going from unaware to aware, decide, use, and leave.

It is useful to look at human behavior on different levels when working with lifecycles. This is because we all behave differently when we take different roles in relation to a business. In fact, user, customer, consumer, and human mind-sets can coexist at the same time.

As an example, I can behave as a *human* concerned about a stressful move with my family, a smart *consumer* researching the market for a good mortgage deal, a pleased *customer* as I enter into a long-term contract with my preferred bank, and an irritated *user* as I finalize the paperwork online.

Developing a clear overview of how people behave at these four fundamental levels helps to design the service and business most optimally. When you understand customers' experiences in these different roles, you will be better set to focus design solutions on specific hotspots. Being aware of these mind-sets can mean the difference between a growing customer base and a shrinking one.

Human Lifecycle

The human lifecycle describes how people behave in certain stages in life, from childhood to death. It describes typical customer needs and wants in five- to seven-year cycles. The lifecycle at this level focuses on the general human experience, regardless of specific products and services people use.

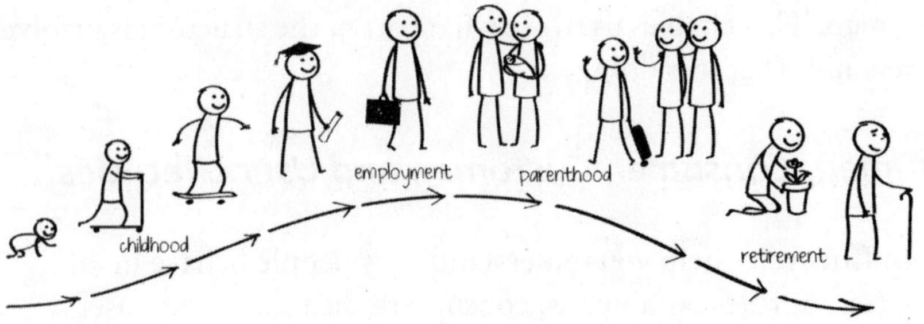

Human lifecycle: *A human lifecycle describes the phases and stages of life and how needs change depending on where people are in their lives. Key to this view are transitions and major life considerations such as leaving home, having a family, or retiring.*

At the human level you get an overview of what really matters in people's lives beyond what your company can offer, and understand demographic trends and changes that affect your business.

The human lifecycle is particularly important for innovation, where companies that discover and meet latent, but undiscovered, needs and motivations can leapfrog competition.

Consumer Lifecycle

The consumer lifecycle describes how people behave in the market when they make choices about how to fulfill their needs and wants. It describes people in situations where they have clearly defined needs but have several options for how they meet them. It describes people's behavior within a marketplace where competitors strive for their attention and also describes how people may get their needs and wants satisfied in completely different ways.

The consumer lifecycle is particularly valuable when you work out how to position your proposition in a sensible way for customers. This will often include how they experience and use your product or service in combination with other products or services—whether they are partners, competitors, or offers with no connection to your company. When you have a clear picture of the customers' situations as they themselves see it, you will be able to meet their needs with precision in a competitive marketplace.

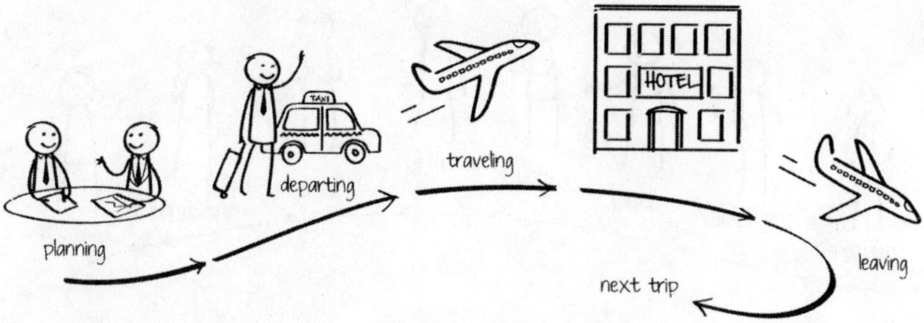

Consumer lifecycle: *A consumer lifecycle describes a consumer activity that will often have multiple services involved. A good example is a business trip or holiday that involves transport, hospitality and other services that come together to create the consumer experience.*

Customer Lifecycle

Customer lifecycles help organizations focus on delivering customer value by structuring the phases of a customer relationship and aligning business processes to the customer experience.

The customer lifecycle helps you find opportunities to do more with people when they make decisions in a paying relationship with the business. It describes how your existing customer decides to buy your product or service, whether to buy more or less, or whether to quit buying altogether.

This lifecycle also gives you a clear overview of the relationships you have with your customers, from awareness to defection. It helps you understand what customers expect from your service and pinpoint how to optimally meet them.

The customer lifecycle is valuable in relationships where the customer—the one who pays—is different from the user, as it helps you understand who to cater to and how to offer the right level of service. This is a typical situation in households where one member buys something and other uses it—a car, train ticket, or insurance package—but even more critical to business in B2B relationships where the contract owner might be far removed from the people who use the service on a daily basis.

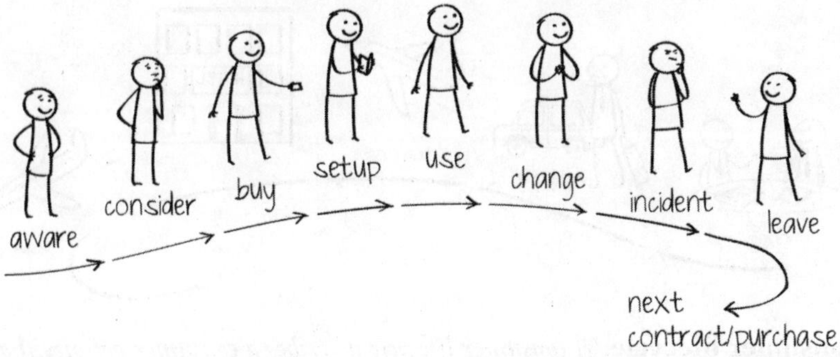

Customer lifecycle: *A customer lifecycle describes how people become customers, their first interactions, regular use, changes and incidents. It is valuable to understand how to gain and keep customers.*

User Lifecycle

The user lifecycle is a great tool to help reduce costs, drive efficiencies, and trigger new behaviors when people use the product or service. It gives you a clear picture of the tasks people do when they interact with your service. It helps you explain how people's needs are met and how your organization helps them solve problems over a period.

This lifecycle helps visualize the journeys people go through during interactions with the business, and how they move across channels from online to phone and face-to-face to get things done.

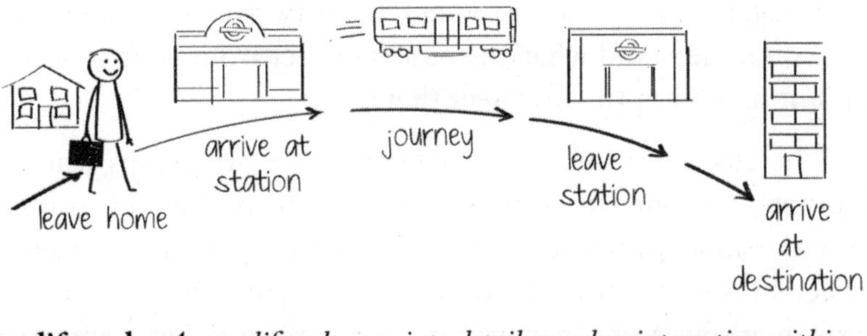

User lifecycle: *A user lifecycle goes into detail on a key interaction within a service. This could be a regular task or activity such as checking your bank status or using a railway station. User lifecycles focus on how customers achieve one or everyday tasks.*

The user lifecycle is extremely powerful for getting an outside-in picture of service delivery in order to renew, simplify, and improve. It helps highlight gaps between customer needs and system capabilities—and gives you information on how to fix them. It also enables you to simplify complex problems, as it often reveals systems and processes that provide little customer value. Ultimately, it helps you focus on the functions and features that really make a difference to customers.

Takeaway Messages

1. Lifecycles are extremely powerful tools to understand customer behavior and identify business opportunities.
2. Use the human lifecycle to spot gaps in the market and innovate new propositions.
3. The consumer lifecycle allows you to understand how people make choices and design ways to support them to make the right choices.
4. The customer lifecycle enables you to optimize the contract-holding experience and increase customer value and loyalty.
5. The user lifecycle gives you an outside-in picture of service delivery in order to simplify and improve customer interactions.

The Front-Stage and the Back-Stage of the Customer Experience

Align the channels customers see "front-stage" with internal processes "back-stage" to simplify the experience and reduce complexity in the organization.

A service design approach offers ways to align the organization and business capabilities with customers' needs, wants, and experiences. The key is to look at the business in terms of front-stage and back-stage design. This gives you a visual overview and helps you gain greater clarity on the things that affect your customer's experience.

Front-stage views encompass all the things the business does that customers can see, hear, feel, and touch. These customer "touchpoints" typically include staff behavior, websites, call centers, printed material, marketing, and products.

Back-stage views comprise all the things the business does that are invisible to customers, but essential to enable the customer experience. This can include how departments are organized and business capabilities such as enterprise IT systems, routines, and many other things.

Service design explores both front-stage and back-stage from a customer perspective. How do customers experience the sum of front-stage parts in their relationship with the service provider, and how are customers affected by the way your company has designed its internal processes and systems?

When you start to design the front-stage and back-stage from the outside in, you will often uncover astonishing opportunities to reduce complexity and simplify the organization.

Front-Stage

Mapping front-stage touchpoints will help to get a full outside-in picture of what customers might see when they engage with the service. When mapped across the customer journey, it also reveals how different touchpoints can meet diverse needs in a range of situations for customers.

The first thing the front-stage view will do is to help people inside your organization gain a shared picture of how the service is experienced by customers. Usually, different silos are responsible for different touchpoints, and it can be difficult to see how services provided by one department affect others. Seeing how all the touchpoints work together from a customer perspective is a powerful way to eliminate turf wars and misunderstandings.

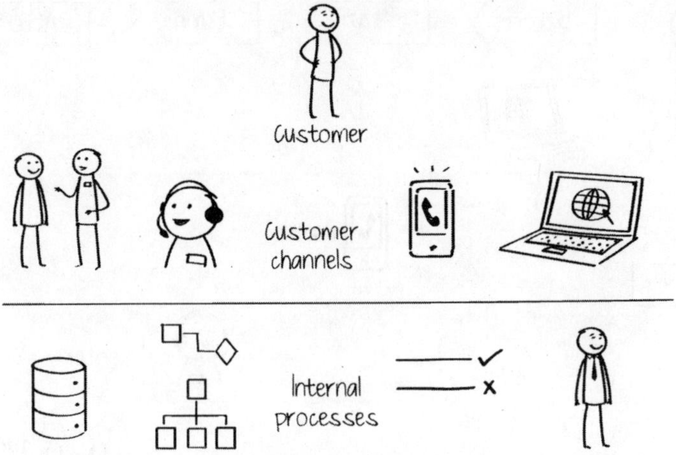

Front-stage, back-stage: *An example of mapping front-stage touchpoints with the organization and capabilities back-stage.*

The great potential for a business in gaining clarity on the "front-stage" is to use the insight to work systematically to align touchpoints. Identify which touchpoints serve customers best, in which situations and in combination with other touchpoints. This exercise makes it possible to eliminate waste when several touchpoints unnecessarily overlap to offer customers service when they are perfectly well served by one. As an example, a telco had sales teams for retail, phone, and online shops, but all had different systems to store sales history. By sharing one system, they were able continue a sales dialogue across all channels and close the sale when it was right for the customer.

A clear front-stage picture is likely to reveal typical customer irritations and faults where the service drops customers between touchpoints. In some situations it will even help to see exactly where you lose customers through poor service alignment. The front-stage view enables you to optimize particular touchpoints for high-value customer interactions and design touchpoints to serve customers in the right combination. This helps to ensure customers feel engaged in rich and memorable experiences in costly channels as well as enabled to self-serve in volume in low-cost channels.

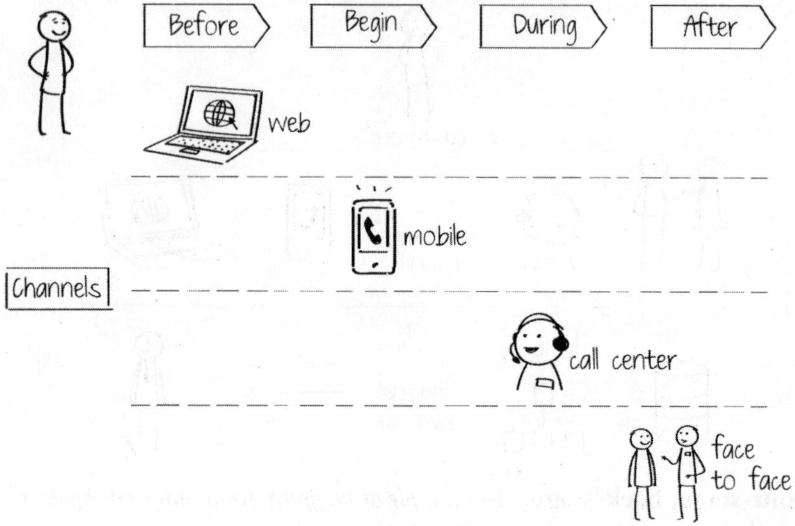

Front-stage: *The front-stage describes customer needs, experiences, and the channels or touchpoints used to engage them by a service organization.*

The real business value of the front-stage view comes to fruition when you use it to systematically design how customers migrate from one channel to another through the customer journey to reduce costs or increase revenues. Perhaps you want to move customers from the web to phone to finally commit a new customer to a sale, or use the call center actively to teach customers to self-serve in low-value transactions.

The front-stage service view gives you visibility of the way the service meets customers, enables you to control how touchpoints align, and ultimately how you can manage customers in any channel.

Back-Stage: Organization

When you have a clear picture of the service front-stage, you can map how different departments in the organization align to deliver one, consistent customer experience. The back-stage view provides a picture of how departments align to the customer journey and to the front-stage touchpoints. It shows which parts of the organization are active in specific customer interactions and how they need to coordinate actions.

The organizational view makes it clear who actually does what to deliver the service to customers. It highlights opportunities to align departments better to deliver in the most effective way. In some cases, seeing the way departments are organized from a customer perspective helps simplify organizational structures.

A critical organizational view allows us to analyze the potential impact of changes to the way the service is delivered to customers. A seemingly small improvement to the customer may impact a department beyond any expectation or lead to serious challenges in the way silos coordinate their operations. When you connect back-stage concerns to the front-stage customer experience, you can see, discuss, and often resolve undesired consequences of customer experience redesign. The earlier telco example is a case in point. A sales bonus structure rewarding staff for sales in their own channel posed a major hurdle for implementing a shared sales system. Seeing how this policy actually prevented a customer-friendly sales process, performance indicators were changed to reward staff also for sales in other channels.

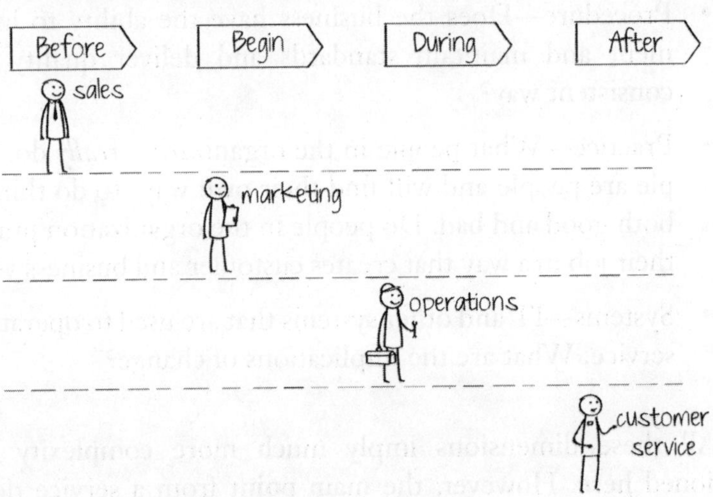

Back-stage organization: *The back-stage organization is the teams, departments, or functions that together deliver the service.*

Getting a clear view of the back-stage helps people in different departments see what they need to deliver and to agree to deliver the right things with the customer in mind.

Back-Stage: Business Capabilities

The back-stage of the service involves other dimensions that are essential to success with customers. This view enables you to map capabilities that cross the organization and impact on the customer experience—including capabilities like:

- People—How do members of an organization behave as individuals and as a group? Do you need to make changes with staff behavior?
- Policy—Do the principles that guide decision making in the business lead to the right customer experience—and do employees adhere to them?
- Process—Are processes designed to serve customers well or do they serve internal purposes that provide little customer value?
- Procedure—Does the business have the ability to implement and maintain standards and deliver quality in a consistent way?
- Practice—What people in the organization *really* do. People are people and will find their own ways to do things—both good and bad. Do people in the organization practice their job in a way that creates customer and business value?
- Systems—IT and other systems that are used to operate the service. What are the implications of change?

All these dimensions imply much more complexity than mentioned here. However, the main point from a service design perspective is to gain a visual overview of how things connect, from customer touchpoints to operations deep in the engine room of the business. An overview of the front-stage and back-stage enables a controlled approach to service redesign and improvement.

Mapping back-stage capabilities provides clarity and helps to prioritize what creates most value for customers. It also enables you to identify the capabilities that make the greatest difference, which in turn helps drive efficiency. Getting a clear overview of the connection between the front-stage touchpoints and the capabilities helps to determine the right system to develop to help customers get a job done.

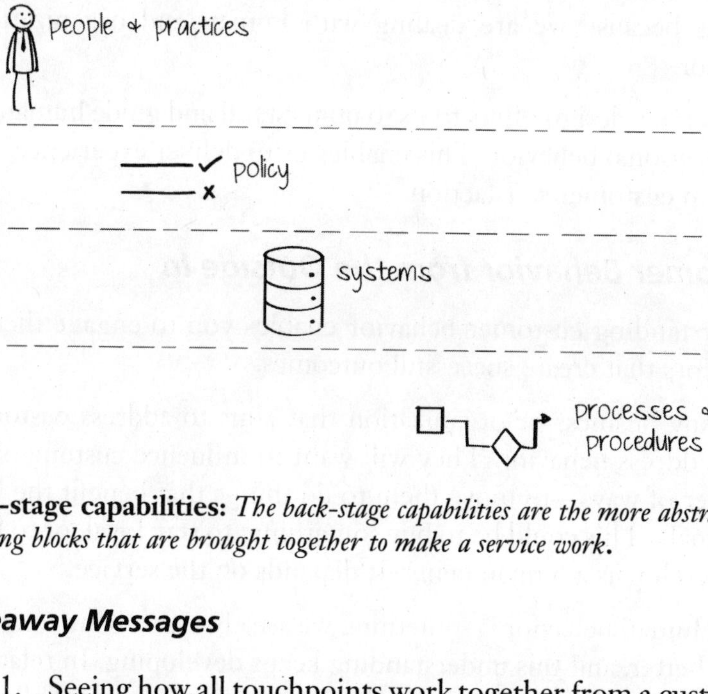

Back-stage capabilities: ***The back-stage capabilities are the more abstract building blocks that are brought together to make a service work.***

Takeaway Messages

1. Seeing how all touchpoints work together from a customer perspective is a powerful way to eliminate turf wars and misunderstandings.
2. The front-stage service view gives you visibility of the way the service meets customers and enables you to control how touchpoints align.
3. The back-stage view lets you see how internal business processes affect customers' experience.

4. Eliminate waste when channels unnecessarily overlap to offer customers service when they are perfectly well served by one.
5. Seeing how front-stage and back-stage align enables a controlled approach to service redesign and improvement.

BEHAVIOR

Movement and structure provide a framework for understanding and designing services, but what happens in reality is far messier. This is because we are dealing with human and organizational behavior.

Service design offers tools to understand and guide human and organizational behavior. This enables us to deliver experiences that result in customer satisfaction.

Customer Behavior from the Outside In

Understanding customer behavior enables you to engage them in behaviors that create successful outcomes.

Any business or organization that aims to address customers must address behavior. They will want to influence customers in a number of ways—to move them to do things that benefit the business goals. This could be to buy something, to stay loyal, or to learn and develop as a human being. It depends on the service.

Human behavior is something we are always striving to understand better, and this understanding keeps developing. In relatively recent years, the discipline of behavioral economics has challenged more traditional views on how people behave, questioning how rational we really are, and helping us understand why people do things that seem illogical. A great example for service design is the theory that people fail to fully consider their future selves and therefore do not make decisions that have high future benefit in favor of shorter-term value.

A service design approach has a specific take on behavior and how we can understand it better for the purpose of creating

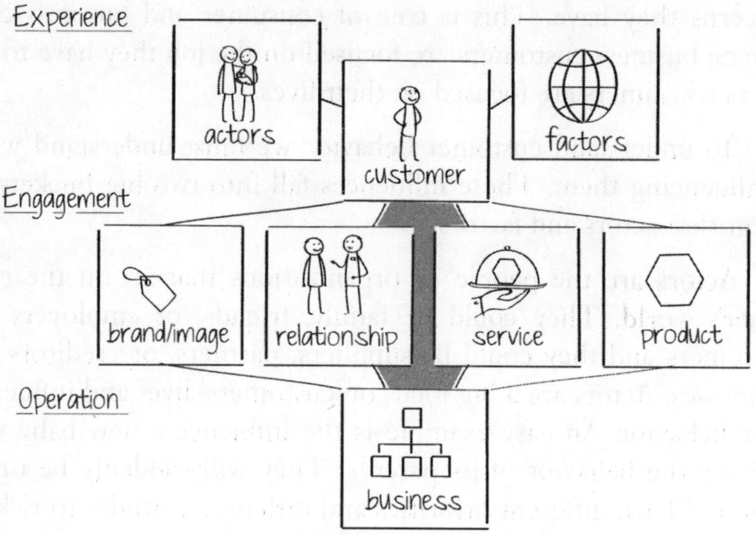

Outside-in: *The external actors and factors in a customer's world relate to their experience and to the tools used to engage them by service organizations.*

higher-performing services. This view starts with the understanding that businesses and customers are very different entities and have very different motivations and goals. There is a tension between the two. Customers may be concerned with their day-to-day lives and jobs while businesses have their strategies and practices. Different motivations mean different behaviors and a lack of understanding between the two. Service design aims to provide a better translation and alignment by bringing insight into customer behavior into the way an organization behaves when it engages customers.

Actors and Factors Influence Customer Behavior

We have to see people, who may be customers, from the outside of the organizations and businesses we work for to fully understand them. Unless we do, their actions will be misunderstood. People—consumers, customers—are rarely sitting around waiting to use our services. They are busy with their lives and the primary concerns they have. This is true of consumer and business customers; business customers are focused on the job they have to do just as consumers are focused on their lives.

To understand customer behavior we must understand what is influencing them. These influences fall into two big buckets or categories: actors and factors.

Actors are the people or organizations that are in the customer's world. They could be family, friends, or employers for consumers and they could be suppliers, partners, or creditors for businesses. Actors are a big focus on customers' lives and influence their behavior. An easy example is the influence a new baby will have on the behavior of its parents. They will suddenly be time-poor and have different priorities and different attitudes to risk or entertainment. The same is true of a business where a key actor such as their bank will have a strong influence on their decisions and actions.

A factor is something that has influence on customers but is more abstract. It could be a trend such as demographic change or a law or even the weather. These are things that influence behavior and can be considered in service design. A good example is congestion in a city and how it influences our decisions about when and how to travel. A regular example is government policy and how that influences behavior as people or businesses must comply with laws and regulations.

Understanding actors and factors is critical to putting yourself in the customer shoes and seeing why they behave in certain ways.

Stages of the Lifecycle and Behavior

After exploring outside actors and factors, we can step closer to how a customer behaves in relation to a particular service or sector. Now customers are influenced by where they are in their lifecycle. There will be times where they have high need and high attention to a service and times when they do not. This will depend on whether they have a high need to sign a new contract or resolve an issue or if things are ticking along and their attention is elsewhere.

Interestingly, we often see a mismatch between customer attention, need, and business engagement. When customer needs are high, business engagement is low. Three key examples of this are when customers are considering a service, setting it up, or need to change their use. These are points where the customer has a high need for support to get things right for them but the business motivation to support them is lower. Setup is a good example as a service has just made a sale, has a new customer, and moves on to the next. However, the customer is left with a new service that they have yet to fully understand or integrate into their lives. This can cause them to misuse it, demand more support as they do not understand, or try to leave at the first opportunity as they feel they bought the wrong thing. These are all behaviors that can be understood by using a lifecycle view.

Experiences Influence and Behavior

Moving in from the outside world of the customer, through the lifecycle stages they are in, to the actual experiences they have, we get another view on customer behavior. This is the most recognized and commonly discussed: the customers' response to experiences. People behave in reaction to their environment. If they are frustrated, they will complain or seek to go elsewhere. If they are unable to complete, a task they will give up. If the rules are too rigid, they may cheat.

Engaging with customers and understanding the experience they have interacting with services enables us to instantly see why they do the things they do. More importantly, it helps to see how we could engage them differently and enable them to do what would be better for them and for our businesses. In this way service design differs from other responses to customer behavior in that it seeks to enable rather than seduce or coerce. There is longer-term and more sustainable benefit in supporting customers to achieve their goals and complete their tasks.

Takeaway Messages

1. Understand the actors and factors that influence customer behavior.
2. Look at how lifecycle stages impact on what customers need.
3. Dive into the specifics on customer experience to see why they do the things they do.

Business Behavior from the Inside Out

> There is a tension between businesses and organizations and customers that must be acknowledged to understand how businesses behave toward customers.

This tension has three key dynamics. First, that business goals can differ from customer goals so there is a natural, healthy, tension between motivations. Second, most businesses aim to scale and service significant numbers of customers and must standardize and drive efficiency, whereas customers are individuals who want their specific needs addressed. Third, the people in organizations live in the organizational world where their primary concerns are around colleagues, hierarchies, and structures that are of no relevance to customers. These three factors hugely influence business behavior and the behavior that customers experience.

The motivational tension means that businesses will behave in their interests, and customers will be suspicious of this. This applies to both private and public sectors.

The scale and efficiency tension means that businesses will tend toward treating customers en masse and designing engagements that aim to manage the demand. Customers can then feel that the business is impersonal and mechanical.

The inside/outside tension leads to strange customer experiences where they get to see the structures of the company as they are passed from one department to another or lost in transition. The service follows the organizational design rather than the customer journey.

These tensions must be recognized to understand how business behavior impacts customer experience. What is also important to understand is that the focus on how businesses engage customers influences their behavior.

Product-Driven Behaviors

One key factor that influences business behavior and is particularly pertinent to services is product. By this, we mean that the industrial concept of a product has defined the makeup of businesses, what they do, and how they conduct themselves. Product thinking focuses on the manufacture and sale of products and aims to do this as efficiently as possible. This applies not only to manufacturers but also to service sector companies where the product is intangible, like a mortgage or a gas supply.

Product thinking focuses on defining a specific customer need and meeting it with a clearly defined and controlled thing. This tends to neglect the needs that surround the product—from the need to understand and choose the right product to the need to dispose of it when it is redundant.

The behavior that product thinking creates in business is a neglect of the services that surround the product and missed opportunities. It means that products get a lot of promotion, but how they are chosen and installed comes a far second. It fails to support all customers' needs through the lifecycle.

Brand-Driven Behaviors

Along with product, brand is a major tool in customer engagement and a factor in how businesses behave. A brand is designed to communicate the value and values of the organization to customers, to set expectations, and to make a promise. It is also a face for the organization that defines how customers should expect it to behave. Some brands aim to be friendly, others to be reassuringly formal.

A brand may be incredibly strong and carry huge equity and value with customers so that it can define the principles of behavior for products and services. Its limits are in its strength. In being unifying and holistic, it can neglect the details of human interactions.

Service-Driven Behaviors

Service should be understood as how we interact with customers through the customer lifecycle, from their first awareness through becoming customers, onboarding, using and reconsidering, or changing. Service behaviors differ from product or brand in that they follow the customers through the processes they need to go through to achieve their goals. Service performance is different because the focus is on achieving specific outcomes for customers.

Takeaway Messages

1. Recognize the tension between customer and organizations and how this influences business behavior.
2. Understand that product, brand, and service are different devices to engage customers and encourage different business behaviors.

CHALLENGES

Applying the Foundations to Business Challenges

The following chapters take a business challenge and explore how to approach it using a service design approach. These chapters cover challenges in three areas, *the customer story*, *business impact*, and *organizational challenge*.

Each chapter sets the business context and what the challenge is before defining how a service design approach can be applied.

To do this, we have illustrated approaches that can be used in the specific challenge. These approaches use the concepts introduced in the foundation section.

Each approach uses the *movement*, *structure*, and *behavior* framework to illustrate how to tackle the challenge. This means that we align our concerns, whether they are customer experiences or business impacts, to a lifecycle of customer journey that defines the *movement* in each case. To keep things simple we have used either the story structure of *before*, *begin*, *during*, and *after*, or a generic set of stages of a lifecycle that defines high-level steps a customer must take, such as *aware*, *consider*, *buy*, and *setup*, that outline a typical *before* to *begin* customer journey.

The approaches differ more in the *structures* used in each case. These are the considerations that are mapped to the *movement* and could be done with the customer, the business, or the organization. For example, in *the customer story* chapter, the structures are how to understand and map customer experiences and engagement activities. In *business impact*, the structures are more about the business benefits, outcomes, and goals—and for *organizational challenge*, the

Challenge framework: *Each challenge used the framework of movement, structure, and behavior to illustrate how to approach a service design challenge.*

structure represents aspects of the organization, such as functions or capabilities.

Within these structures we illustrate the behaviors that can take place. This may be the actions of the customer, business, or organization. The behaviors are simplified to help get the point across.

Visit www.liveworkstudio.com/SDforB to learn more about supporting approaches and case studies.

Chapter 3

The Customer Story

Understanding Customers Better Provides the Basis for Customer-Driven Service Improvement and Innovation

Customers have stories—stories about what they are doing in their lives, about their work, leisure, and journeys. These stories have highs and lows and make up the experiences of life. Customer stories—their experiences—are impacted by the services they use, whether it is the bus to work, the hospital visit, or the insurance claim while on holiday.

Customer stories cut through the jargon of business, even the jargon of customer experience and service design, and focus on people and the things that improve their lives and work—things that add value.

Understanding customer stories also helps service providers to think about what story they want customers to tell about their experience with the organization. Will the story be positive, will they recommend you, or will they complain?

First, service design offers businesses or service providers an approach to understand and capture customers' stories in ways that make their experience easier to understand. Second, service design methods enable businesses to develop new stories about how they can provide better services.

This section of the book focuses on these two aspects of service design. It will help you introduce these methods into your organizational practice and guide you in how to use them to inform service improvement and innovation. We look specifically at the challenge of *customer experience excellence* and how to approach it. Then we look at dealing with *irritations* and *failures* for customers and the impact they can have. We move on to look at how to better *engage customers* and finally get more ambitious and start to look at the challenge of *innovating* new service propositions.

GET THE BASICS RIGHT AND ACHIEVE CUSTOMER EXPERIENCE EXCELLENCE

A growing number of organizations are beginning to understand that customer experience is a critical business factor. Commercial businesses in competitive markets can see how easily customers who've had poor experiences choose to switch to another provider.

Governments realize that good "customer" experience goes hand in hand with a more efficient and effective public service. However, many organizations find it hard to move from understanding the importance of an excellent customer experience to actually delivering one.

In approaching customer experience, many organizations rely on feedback from surveys and panels to listen to customers, or use methods such as Net Promoter Score to identify areas of improvements. Service design goes beyond asking customers for feedback by taking a holistic customer experience perspective; it involves learning what customers experience when they consider your product, buy your service, interact with your organization, receive a competitive offer, or find an alternative solution. Understanding what moves customers in these situations, how they made choices, and what influences their path provides the insight that you can build on to improve these experiences for customers and improve business performance.

INSIGHTS

- Businesses struggle to know what their strategy is for customer experience and can get seduced by creating magic moments that do not impact performance. Focusing on brilliant basics is essential, as customers do not appreciate the magic if the basics are broken. Magic moments will emerge, and the best ones are low cost.
- It is easy for businesses to think that they need to change *what* they offer to improve the experience, and this implies hard rewiring of the organization. Often the bigger impact is in changing *how* you offer and deliver what you already have. Outside-in can be as simple as changing terminology so customers understand or improving basic touch-points such as contracts and invoices.

(continued)

(continued)

- Customer experience excellence risks being seen as in opposition to cost control—it can be seen as a luxury. The best approach is to align customer experience excellence with business performance and aim to drive both in parallel. A good experience should reduce costs or grow revenues.

Why Read On?

- Learn how to structure customer experience insights.
- Understand what a truly outside-in view looks like.
- Develop a systematic approach to experience improvement.

Customer Experience Excellence

What is customer experience excellence? Words like easy, smooth, flow, painless, effortless, and helpful help to define the concept. Another set of words that we hear less frequently but that gets a lot of attention includes terms like delightful, surprising, fun, meaningful, or even amazing. We can think of an excellent experience in these two ways—as a mix of getting the basics right and doing something special. Experience shows that there is little point in doing the second if the first lets you down, as customers tend to remember the bad more than the good.

Services with large numbers of customers, like banks, are regularly run by a set of hard rules. Customers can find themselves penalized for doing something that they do not feel was wrong—like being overdrawn when they have lots of money in a parallel savings account. This kind of irritation causes high levels of stress and frustration that are hard to counter with bribes and special offers. However, it would be excellent if the bank was able to see that overall the customer is in good standing and forgives him or her.

There are various reasons why delivering an excellent customer experience is challenging. One is that customer experience is a new priority requiring new skills, understanding, and investment. Another reason is that real customer experience excellence requires viewing everything the organization does differently. For organizations that have traditionally been internally focused, truly approaching business from the outside in, from the customer's perspective—rather than from the inside out—is a major change and more radical than it sounds.

An excellent customer experience can have a positive impact on a range of key performance indicators (KPIs) from *acquisition* to *retention* by way of *cost to serve*. Removing barriers (irritations) that customers encounter makes it easier for them to buy a service, and preventing any hurdles removes motivations to switch. Delivering magic moments (delights) when it really matters to customers and creating a positive experience will lead to them recommending your service to others. Recommendation and customer promotion of a service is invaluable.

How to Understand Your Organization from the Outside-In

To get an understanding of *irritations* that stand in the way of delivering an excellent experience or *delights* that make it memorable, it is essential to start with the customer. Understanding the outcomes that motivate the customer and determining how to help them achieve these goals is key to delivering a great experience.

To many organizations, looking at their services and their organization from the outside-in means putting on hold all those noisy, important business goals and *listening* closely to figure out what the customer wants to achieve. This often leads to some hard truths as teams discover that, "we are not as important to customers as we thought we were—they don't really care," and "gosh, we make it really hard for our customers to do simple things like buy our products." These truths are essential in discovering what excellence looks like for customers—and helps businesses uncover valuable insights about what irritates and delights customers.

This outside-in view can draw on a wide range of insight into customer experience from survey data to qualitative research such as customer shadowing or in-depth interviews. It is essential to structure your understanding of the service from the customers' perspective—not the business process view. This means defining the activities and needs that customers have step-by-step. Take a simple example, the experience of buying something. As a customer, I need to be *aware* of a product or nothing will happen, then I need to *understand* what it is and the benefits it may offer me, then I need to *consider* whether I want it or not. Then I have to *buy* it. If I am not able to complete any of these tasks I cannot move forward and the sale is not complete. Thinking about what a customer needs at each of the stages helps us to restructure our thinking and potentially design a better sales approach. This can differ from product to product—some need greater *consideration* than others. With complex machinery, many sales fail due the lack of support to customers in their *consideration* of what their best solution is.

This step-by-step structuring of an experience in terms of the outcomes that customers *must* achieve to move forward can be applied to all aspects of experience, not just purchase. A service design approach would look at delivery, complaints, retention, and more in the same structured way—always through the customers' eyes and in their shoes.

Gaining this kind of insight into customers is a simple thing but surprisingly difficult to do in a large organization. Watching customers interact with your organization will give you a different perspective. Asking them about their experience using a structured interview that captures their story will provide insight that was never given through the day-to-day interactions you have with customers. It is surprisingly difficult because it is time out from day-to-day tasks, and you have to listen well and only ask questions that keep the customer talking. This is hard for people who care about their business, as it can mean listening to painful truths.

Revealing truths and using *customer stories* helps organizations understand customer experiences—and it helps teams move logically through a process of creating ideas, testing options, and detailing solutions. Visualization tools, such as storyboards, visual maps, and prototypes make interactions between service providers and customers more tangible—and enable services to be tested, discussed, and improved.

Approaches for Understanding Experiences

1. **Enabling customer flow**

   Movement through stages of a service moves customers toward the goals we have hired the service to enable customers to achieve. Movements can be the small everyday things like buying a coffee or a metro ticket, or bigger things such as getting medical treatment. Whether large or small, customers need to progress, or flow, with minimal barriers or hurdles to navigate. There are two factors in customers achieving their goals: their motivations, the *drivers* that are pushing them to pursue their goals, and the *hurdles* they encounter on the journey. If the hurdles are larger than the drivers, then customers will give up or fail.

Drivers and hurdles: *This diagram shows how we can map drivers and hurdles as side-by-side factors in the phases of customers' movement through a service. This example describes an abstracted experience through a purchase of a product or service and how customer motivations can be easily thwarted.*

2. **Equating customer flow to business performance**

   No business will invest in customer experience without an idea of what that investment delivers back. Luckily, mapping the opportunities we identify to deliver customer experience excellence enables us to map the business benefits—what we get if the customer is successful. Enabling the customer to smoothly move through the phases of the customer experience also enables the business to realize value in ways that map directly to the customers' experience.

Opportunity and value: *The same framework that we used to map barriers and hurdles can be used to define opportunities to improve the benefit for the business.*

How to Develop and Deliver Customer Excellence in Practice

Insurance is not a desired product—it is required by law or a begrudged cost—and therefore a challenging space to design excellent customer experiences. Insurance companies have few ways to engage their customers in positive experiences and build loyalty, so they must do as much as they can with the interactions they do have.

An insurer that understood the importance of customer experience to its business found that by focusing on the customer basics—such as being easy to buy from, setting customers up to understand their coverage, making it easy for them to change their contract terms and to resolve any issue—it was able to remove any irritations and steadily rise up the ranking for customer satisfaction nationwide. They moved from outside the top 50 to inside the top 10 alongside more desirable propositions such as luxury cars and holiday travel. The insurer targeted customer experience excellence because highly satisfied customers spend significantly more with them.

In addition to focusing on getting the basics right, the insurer focused on delivering a magic moment around the one real moment of truth in the insurance business: a claim. By talking to customers who had recently made a claim and by listening in on customer claims calls, they were able to understand the journey from the outside-in. What they learned was that customers have significant emotional needs from the claim experience as well as the transactional need. If they have suffered a theft or a loss, perhaps abroad, their stress levels are high.

Think of a family on holiday that has had an accident and needs help with foreign medical services and then to get back home. This is a crisis for the family; however, it's a daily occurrence for those who designed the processes and manned the phones. Rethinking and redesigning this experience so that the staff really listened to customers and helped them in their hour of need gave a small, but significantly engaged, number of customers a real reason to believe in the firm as a trustworthy partner in their lives. One customer having experienced the new claims process went as far as to say, "Whatever we are paying you, it's worth it!"

Our insurer was able to make this an excellent experience by identifying an opportunity to delight customers and really caring for them at a moment of emotional need. This was invaluable in a sector with very little opportunity to connect to customers at this level.

Takeaway Messages

1. An excellent experience is 90 percent brilliant basics and 10 percent magic moments.
2. Getting the basics right impacts on business performance, from acquisition to retention.
3. Delivering magic moments impacts on reputation and word of mouth promotion.
4. Revealing truths and using *customer stories* helps organizations understand customer experiences—and it helps teams move logically through a process of creating ideas, testing options, and detailing solutions.

PREVENT CUSTOMER IRRITATIONS AND FAILURES

Talk to most people about services and customer experience—from financial services, telecoms, and utilities to health care or the government tax office—and they will tell you a story of an experience they had that was irritating. But customers across the world are less and less willing to put up with such irritations in their day-to-day lives. This is partly due to empowered consumers and individuals, partly due to the good examples set by some leading companies, and partly due to technologies showing customers that things can be different.

A service design approach, starting from the outside in, often begins by identifying irritations that businesses did not know existed (because they never asked). Once you have heard the same irritation story from a number of customers, service design has the tools to define the solution.

INSIGHTS

- Single irritations can seem small and immaterial. Businesses that successfully address irritations take an *incremental gains* philosophy that sees each irritation as perhaps 1 percent of the problem so that 20 resolved irritations can be seen as a significant 20 percent improvement.
- Resolving irritations is not sexy. This agenda can struggle to compete with more visionary strategies. It is advisable to use the strong voice of the customer tools like videos of customers explaining their pains to drive home how frustrated customers are and keep the agenda real.

Why Read On?

- Learn how to identify and resolve irritations and failures.
- Understand how irritations are a complex mix of emotions.
- See how to prioritize and validate fixes.

Customer Irritations and Failures

An irritation is a long wait, having to repeat yourself, or needing to call or find someone when a website or machine is too difficult to use. Irritations lead to additional costs somewhere along the line as customers complain, seek help, seek redress for a mistake, or simply complain to their friends and colleagues. They cause waste work and erode reputations. A failure, however, is something more: it is what happens when customers cannot achieve the task that they set out to complete or address a particular need. Perhaps they cannot buy something they were looking for, or do not get the service they have paid for—or more significantly, they can't access essential maintenance, care, or advice. Service failures might lead the customers somewhere else, or cause them to suffer a more significant impact on their lives. Understanding irritations or failures from the customers' perspective provides insight into how issues can be addressed and avoided.

One fantastic example is of a high-end hotel where a lot of money and attention has gone into the quality of the service, from the impeccable staff to the stylish bar. However, some customers happen to check in at 5 a.m. and are greeted with a hefty *early check-in* fee. This irritation, that they probably have to accept, puts the rest of the stay under a cloud.

Whether a minor irritation or a major failure, customer issues are important to businesses. It may be that your brand and customer base is slowly eroded as each little irritation leads customers to complain, adding to your cost to serve. It may be that more significant failures are actually impacting your ability to acquire or retain customers. And major failures could impact your reputation and brand.

How to Understand and Systematically Eliminate Irritations

Irritations and failures often go unseen. Businesses are so often focused on their operations that they become oblivious to the customer's part in the successful delivery of their services. For example, a major U.K. utility business only knew that they were failing to connect new customers when their complaints queue grew so long that they investigated the cause—many hundreds of irritated customers later.

Complaints are a good starting point to understand customer irritations. However, they only represent the tip of the iceberg—the customer who actually bothers to find a phone number and make the call. Complaints are generally linked to the things that customers really need to resolve their issue. Irritations that cause customers to simply give up on you—either give up buying or give you less business—are often unreported. There are other sources that help you to get to the less-accessible and potentially more valuable insights into irritations and failures.

A lot of insight can be gained from engaging staff. Many large organizations do not tap the gold mine that is the knowledge and experience of their employees. Employees are in daily direct contact with customers—face-to-face, on the phone, or via email—and have an internal database of customer irritations and failures. They may present it as pains that they experience with "difficult" customers, but what they're truly telling you is where the pain points are. There is also significant evidence that if staff are unhappy, customers will be unhappy—because employees tend to receive the brunt of customers' frustrations in their day-to-day work. They want to be able to do their job and help the customer but are sometimes prevented from doing so by the organization's systems or processes. The "computer says no" phenomenon is a perfect example of this—organizational systems prevent staff from helping customers, a scenario that frustrates both parties.

A lot of insight leaves a business when its disgruntled customers do. One point at which customers are particularly clear on the specific irritation or failure that broke the deal occurs when they make a conscious decision to leave. Simply recording these reasons as—or after—customers leave is a second well-employed source of insight.

"Walking in the customer's shoes" is an invaluable way to gather insight into irritations. You can shadow customers in specific aspects of their experience and observe customer interactions with different touch-points in your service. This approach can be combined with a mix of real-life research—eyeballs on the ground watching—and more technologically enabled methods that utilize phone or digital channels. Shadowing gives you the specific moments of customer failure in a specific process. The eyeballs will enable you to see *why* the failure happens, what the customer issue is, and how hard they have to work to resolve it. Finally, it is important to talk to customers and understand their feelings in their own words. Ultimately, irritation is an emotion, and it can be this key factor that is lost in more quantitative methods of research.

These sources of insight become especially powerful when they are brought together in the customer lifecycle framework. Mapping irritations and failures to the phases of the customer lifecycle—the stages through which they must move to achieve their goals—provides structure to your insights, and enables you to manage their prioritization and relate them to root causes.

Approaches for Mapping and Evaluating the Impact of Irritations

1. **Mapping irritations and failures**

   Mapping customers' experiences to a lifecycle provides a repository for the range of insights you have gathered. It lets you correlate insights from different sources and evaluate their severity. There are many ways to represent experiences throughout the lifecycle; we can pinpoint what they feel at each stage and where the irritations are at a peak. What is important is to retain the range of insight across these parameters:

   - What are customers doing?
   - What tasks are they undertaking, and how easy are they finding them?

- What are they thinking? Are they conscious of the irritations or on autopilot?
- What are they feeling? Are they highly stressed or relaxed as they feel in control?

All of these insights can be mapped to the lifecycle and provide a picture of where the issues are enabling a more surgical approach to issue resolution.

Thinking, feeling, and doing: *Using our lifecycle view, we can see how to map customer irritations to the stage of the lifecycle where they occur. We can use this framework to capture our customers' insights' into what they are thinking, feeling and doing at each point.*

2. **Evaluating and prioritizing fixes**

   Once you've mapped irritations and failures, they can be evaluated and prioritized. You can then add metrics to create evaluation scores. A customer pain score can be compiled from evaluating the level of irritation and the volume of customers experiencing it. This customer score can then be brought into a prioritization exercise by being balanced against the cost to resolve and the business benefit of resolution.

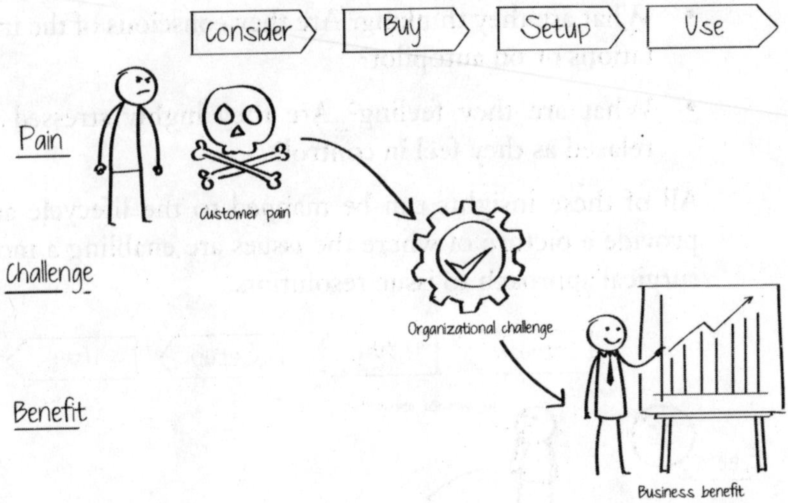

Pain, challenge, and benefit: *Above, we have understood in some detail the nature of the irritation for customers. Below, we show how the same irritation can be assessed in terms of customer pain (take from above) and then balanced against the scale of the challenge to fix the irritation and the potential business benefit in doing so.*

How to Address a Specific Irritation in Practice

A European national railway network was concerned about customer satisfaction levels, having to justify these results to political stakeholders, and suffering bad press.

A small Livework service design team discovered that they were irritating and failing their customers in many, often unknown, ways. They undertook a study to investigate this and garnered some eye-opening results.

Rather than survey customers and rely on their memories of past rail experiences, the team shadowed customers through the full journey—from home to destination—including the **before** and **after** phases when they traveled to and from rail stations. This shadowing took the form of following (with permission) passengers as they bought tickets at machines or ticket windows, navigated stations, rode on trains, and connected to other modes of transport.

By shadowing and observing, the team gained insights into specific irritations and failures that different customer types encountered. For example, watching customers use the machine enabled the team to see that the issue was due to confusion in the language used to describe the tickets to the point where customers were not sure what ticket they were buying. They found that buying a youth card was next to impossible using one of three types of ticket vending machines. They saw how hard older people found reading signage and exiting stations, and they documented more than 100 other issues that customers encountered.

The team used a prioritization methodology that evaluated the level of customer pain, the cost and effort to resolve, and the business value in resolution to give each option a score and enable them to systematically resolve issues, starting with the quick wins and working strategically forward—providing more control over the customer experience program. Some irritations could be validated and fixed overnight, others they had to live with, but now they knew where they stood with customers.

Takeaway Messages

1. Businesses are so often focused on their operations that they become oblivious to the customer's part in the successful delivery of their services.
2. Irritations and failures can be identified through staff, ex-customers, and direct observations.
3. Map irritations and failures to the phases of the customer lifecycle to provide structure to your insights, prioritize fixes, and relate them to root causes.
4. Test fixes to ensure they solve the issue, removing irritations and avoiding failure.

ENGAGE CUSTOMERS EFFECTIVELY

Engaging customers in a way that results in an excellent customer experience is a major challenge for organizations *in every industry*. Engagement is the critical interface between customers and services—it is where experiences are shaped but also where costs are incurred and performance is measured. Both customers and organizations have desired outcomes for each interaction, but these goals are not always aligned.

Service design helps align your engagement approach to customer goals. It also offers methods to develop and test customer engagement approaches in a way that walks the line between customer value and business efficiency. By mapping customer needs to a customer lifecycle or journey and then defining an engagement that will meet these needs, organizations can take control of this challenging task.

INSIGHTS

- Engagement is a useful concept when working with customer-driven approaches. It is often very hard to get people who are deep in the operations of a business to step outside into the world of customer experience. Customer engagement brings insights closer to home as it is about *what do we do to interact with customers?* Most colleagues find this a more accessible conversation.
- Thinking about engagement as "what we do with our customers" can be a useful *plain English term to use with colleagues.*
- Using a customer lifecycle model to catalog all the high-level engagements you have with a customer is a highly useful exercise to understand the bulk of *what you do with customers* and manage decisions about where to focus efforts.

Why Read On?

- Learn how to take action in response to customer experience insights.
- Understand how to change the mode or channel of engagement.
- Develop more effective front office operations.

What Is Customer Engagement?

The customer's goal is primary—it is the reason the service exists—and it is essential that customers are engaged in a way that enables them to succeed. Customer engagement is what businesses, organizations, and service providers do to deliver value to customers. It follows the cycle of the service from *before* the customer begins their relationship with you to when their use of the service *begins,* to what they receive *during* their time as a customer, to *after* they no longer need or want your service. A customer engagement can be a sales activity, a contractual transaction, the delivery of an agreed on or expected service, and the response to a need from the customer. In this way engagement can be an active push out from the organization or the capability to respond to customer demands. Put simply, customer engagement is the front office, front line, or customer-facing activities in any service.

A service design approach to customer engagement helps to tailor the engagement to the experience and needs of the customer—this is different from traditional approaches and provides a more effective way to organize disparate parts of your organization. Take sales, for example. Service design approaches sales as one part of delivering value to customers. A sales experience should leave a customer better informed and better able to make a decision. If it does this, then it has added value. Even if the customer does not buy this time, they may return later.

A good example of this need for balance is low-cost airlines. These companies started out very successfully not through great services but through innovative business processes. The single and compelling value they offered was price. However, as this model matured, the airlines have adapted their strategy and services to accommodate aspects of the customer experience to make their customer engagement smoother and to add value in new areas. Some are hiring service designers to do this. Unless price is the only factor, customer engagement is an essential consideration.

At all times this outside-in perspective must be balanced with inside-out knowledge that recognizes the business priorities and strategies. We are not advocating doing everything the customer asks for, but in most organizations the business perspective needs balancing with a stronger understanding of the customer's experience. This is the tension in service where the customer's needs can be in conflict with the business priorities. The challenge of customer engagement is to deliver services in a way that enables the customers to achieve their goals in the most effective manner for the business.

How to Approach Customer Engagement

Customer engagement should be approached with the question: How do we enable the customers to complete their goals in this interaction effectively? Effectively means in a way that is low effort and low cost for them and for the business. The goal of effective customer engagement is to allow the customers to get back to their lives or business knowing the job has been done. The business benefit will be aligned with the customer need, so a better sales experience should lead to more sales but also higher sales efficiency.

As with any service design activity, defining the best approach to customers' engagement starts with understanding customers' experiences and needs at each stage of their journey as customers. This is done by gathering data about customer experiences, behaviors, needs, and motivations. It is helpful to use the customer journey structure to organize your data and insights. Think of engagement as the response to understanding that need. If customers need to understand and decide, as in the sales example, then the engagement approach should support them to do so. At this point it is necessary to go deeper into the customer need and ask a range of questions to understand the specifics of the need. These questions can be asked directly of customers who have been through the experience but even better should be asked through observation of customers undertaking the task itself. What people remember is different from what they actually did. Both forms of insight are valid, one to understand the immediate experience, the other to understand the longer-term impact through what they retained in memory. A healthy mix of the two is always a good idea.

What information do customers need to understand the service? If it is to understand, then what information do they need to do that, what is the best way to get that information to them, what language should be used to ensure that they understand the information (often not the language used within the service organization)?

Take a different example that, like sales, is about customers' understanding. When people travel to a new place, they need to understand the public transport system, specifically the ticketing.

Every city has a slightly different ticketing system, and generally the system does not help visitors understand how it works. This specific group of customers has an unmet need at this point and could be better engaged as a result of understanding that need. Perhaps there can be a special advice area for visitors at key entrance points to the city such as airports and major stations. The value of this engagement is clear. Visitors are able to use the service now that they understand how to pay for it.

A key aspect of customer engagement is selection of the right mode or channel used to engage customers. Often business drivers looking for efficiency through channel shifts drive these decisions. A service design approach looks at the mix of channels together as the means of engagement and optimizes this mix. Customer engagement can quickly become about channels: what channels to use to engage customers and how to implement in the channel. Before doing this it helps to establish channel-neutral principles about how you want to engage customers in response to the target experience you wish to support. These principles will then provide a useful quality check against any channel specific plans. For example, the principle could be to translate technical terms into customer language. The channel approach may then mean changing call-center scripts.

Customers do not think about making channel choices in the way that businesses do. They think about the needs or tasks they have and the best way to achieve them. If they fail or are frustrated in one attempt they will try another. Thinking of the channel mix means allowing the channels to play to their strengths and optimize the whole. For example, digital channels are very good for informing customers and enabling transactions and for putting them in control. Human channels, such as retail, are better at providing the empathic advice and support that customers may need at key points.

To engage customers at the right moment, anticipating and meeting customer expectations at each stage of their experience is important. By looking at your service and organization through your customers' eyes, you can discover the engagement moments, or touch-points, that are most important to delivering customer experience excellence.

Approaches for Designing Customer Engagement

1. **Designing the customer engagement**

   We can use the mapping approach that plots customers' movement through services to map the needs customers have of services as the basis for designing the engagement. Below is the framework as a starting point. It is essential that, for a specific service, the details behind these headlines are understood.

   - What are the specifics of customers' needs for support with decisions?
   - How can we support customers in a way that enables us to be more effective in sales or ensures that prospective customers make the right decisions?

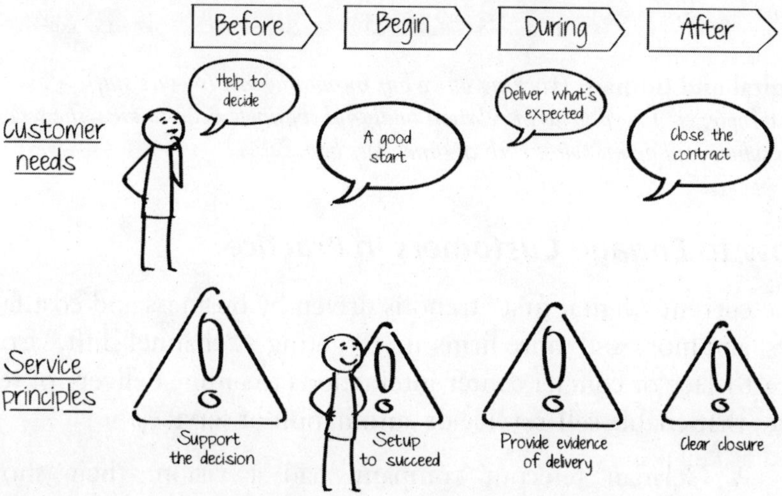

Needs and principles: *Engagement principles should be defined to respond to and address customer needs. They guide the design of the specific mechanism used to meet the needs.*

2. **Engaging across multiple channels**

   Once the engagement principles are clear, we can look at how the channels can work together to deliver on the principle. You can think about the channels as a team, each with a different role supporting the others. This way, rather than separating them into choices for the customer, you create a holistic experience where the customers get what they need through whichever channel they start with.

Digital and human: *Working out what human agents (service staff, salespeople, etc.) need to do in relation to digital channels helps to view the service as a whole and define what each channel does best.*

How to Engage Customers in Practice

The current "digital first" trend is driven by business and cost factors, and more and more firms are targeting a "channel shift," from face-to-face or contact center interactions to online delivery of services that enable self-service or automation of services.

A German telecom company had a vision: their shops and their eshop would work together to create a superior customer experience—where the customer flows, or moves smoothly, between and across channels. The historically separate operations in stores and online would be integrated to provide a consistent experience for customers and also make the most of the qualities of each channel. In the process, the company would create significant business advantage.

To achieve this vision, a cross-functional team investigated the shopping experience of customers and identified the major irritations caused by separate channels and highlighted the opportunities to do more for customers by bringing these channels together. Having identified some key future customer journeys that they believed would win with customers, they designed these journeys in detail. These journeys were service scenarios that described how customers would be engaged through the experience of shopping for a handset and tariff. The strengths of each channel were capitalized on, and at key points devices were designed that would enable customers to cross channels smoothly. For example, customers who began their journey in-store would be able to take an offer home and complete it online. Customers starting online would be able to pick up their order in-store and complete it with a supporting advisor who would ensure their successful setup.

Creating an engagement approach that supported customers through the process and across the channels as a core structure enabled the team to be very clear about what experience they were developing and why. Then they were able to get into the detail of what was required of each channel. This core piece of work provided the strategy to support a range of work streams from development of the ecommerce platform, development of new retail operating model, and retraining of staff.

Takeaway Messages

1. Anticipate and meet customer expectations at each stage of their experience to engage them at the right moment.
2. Look at your service through your customer's eyes to discover engagement moments that are important to deliver an excellent experience.
3. Engagement starts before customers are your customers and ends after optimization.

HIGH-IMPACT CUSTOMER INNOVATIONS

To survive in a competitive market, organizations need to differentiate to stand out. In ambitious businesses there is a strong drive to innovate services that take the organization into new segments or markets. Service design offers a dynamic approach to innovation driven by (unmet) customer needs. What is different about customer innovations is that the goal is to develop new ways of meeting needs rather than improvements or tweaks on the existing model.

In public services, the drive can be to dramatically reduce the cost to serve customers while retaining quality. To do this, it is essential to think radically about how to meet customer needs with significantly fewer or different resources. A customer view is required to be successful. The service design approach develops that customer view to innovate new services or initiate dramatic changes to existing services. It does this in a unique way that starts with customers and connects to business impact and organizational capabilities.

INSIGHTS

- One person's improvement idea is another's innovation concept. Radical has many different interpretations. It is essential to define the innovation goals of your organization before proposing an idea that is either too tame or too radical for your sponsors.
- Innovation is not the day-to-day practice of most people in most organizations. Expecting structured, considered, and well-processed innovation work from teams who have not done it before or are not clearly guided will fail.
- Firsthand observed customer insight is also not regular practice for most organizations—and not something you want to be doing all the time.
- For innovation purposes, insight is fuel for the fire. We are not seeking verifiable truth for all customers; we are looking for the spark that ignites an idea.

Why Read On?

- Learn how to identify unmet customer needs.
- Develop a more tangible way of developing ideas.
- Understand how to build solutions on insights.

Innovating Customer Propositions and Experiences

Innovation in services can be divided into two clear aspects: the customer proposition and the customer experience.

The customer proposition is the offer to customers—it is independent of the experience in that it should be something that is of value above and beyond the specifics of the experience that customers have. However, it is connected, too, the experience must deliver on the proposition. The proposition should be something that is clear, compelling, and a call to action. A proposition has the element of the *elevator* pitch in movies. It should be short, convey the core idea, and make the customer want to investigate further. This is true in commercial or government services. For example, a proposition such as *24/7 access to personal health care* is compelling whether delivered through a hospital or an app. The experience must deliver on this. The access must be easy and the health care must address the specific needs of the patient through the hospital or the app.

Developing and innovating customer propositions and experiences requires insight into customers' deeper needs in ways that move beyond the understanding of their current experience. Looking for opportunities to meet unmet needs or to meet needs in more radically different and efficient ways requires stepping further outside the structures and assumptions of the industry we are working in. A great way to do this is to employ the higher-level lifecycles. To give an example: to innovate in transport, we could look at the customer lifecycle of rail travel. Doing so would probably give us insight into how to make improvements in the experience of rail travel. This may help innovate some specific touch-points in the rail experience (and this is totally valid), but it does not innovate new transport concepts. Looking at the needs people have in the wider lifecycle as a consumer of a range of transport solutions from train to bus to car allows us to find needs and opportunities outside the established models. A great example is the *Kutsuplus* bus service in Finland. This service, a smart mix of a taxi and bus, provides door-to-door service at a greatly reduced cost. The designers of this service spotted an opportunity for low-cost highly convenient service enabled by smart technology that has introduced a new category in a highly conservative industry.

How to Develop Innovative Concepts

Stepping into the human, consumer, or citizen lifecycle and understanding what customers are doing in the lives outside their use of a specific service provides a framework to delve deeper into their needs.

The first option is to look at aspects of the human lifecycle for innovation. This means looking at human needs at key stages in life such as leaving education, starting a family, or retirement. In many cases organizations do not really step outside their business and sector and start with needs at this level. Opportunities from this perspective are exciting as they are independent of existing models. This is truly customer-driven innovation.

The second option is to look at the consumer or citizen lifecycle. By consumer we mean the cycle of satisfying a need within a specific sector (as with the bus example earlier). By citizen we mean the same thing in relation to service provided by government bodies. This level of lifecycle is a great way to look at the options that consumers or citizens have and the choices they make. Often the innovation opportunities can be found in the gaps between different service models or in the edge cases where people have adapted or combined services in new ways that once spotted can be developed into more scalable solutions.

After identifying the opportunities for customer-driven innovation, which come from insight into customers' lives, and uncovering deeper needs outside the everyday services and sectors, the next step is to develop concepts that respond to these opportunities. From concepts, we can progress to marketable propositions through a process of selection, validation, and testing.

Concepts are the precursor of the proposition as we described it. It is an idea that addressed an opportunity space but is independent of the specific execution. A concept is still open to different approaches in execution. This is important, as the specifics of execution could be wrong and kill a concept that is valid.

Defining how to develop an innovative concept requires defining the process that individuals or teams go through to be inspired and spark that breakthrough idea. There are some frameworks that can increase the chances of that spark occurring. The first is to be really clear and specific about the customer lifecycle you are addressing. If, for example, you develop an innovative concept for urban transport, then go to pains to understand the core phases of the personal mobility cycle. Define how the customers you are addressing fix and evolve their transport choices. We have found that people fix their habits and are much more likely to change them when they move home or to a city—this is a key life-cycle element.

Once the lifecycle is understood, then we can drive concepts by creating a contextual structure that runs across the lifecycle. For example, this structure could be different customer groups or behaviors. If we return to the transport example, we could look at how different groups relate to the phase of moving home and establishing new habits. How do students do this and what are their needs—how could we meet these needs in new ways? We could do the same for families and for elderly people and develop three very different concepts based around that one critical phase of the cycle.

Approaches for Developing Concepts

1. **Identifying the opportunities**

   The first step in customer-driven innovation is to understand the market context as experienced by the customer. From the customer perspective we can think of these as "life departments," such as travel, health, or career. This could be a market such as transport as discussed earlier. The context is the activity that the customer is engaged in, which could be moving to a house, raising a family, retirement, or many more. What they have in common is that they are higher-level consumer, citizen, or human lifecycles that take us further into the customers' world.

In relation to this lifecycle, through research and observation, you can identify areas of need and how well that need is being met by existing services. Unmet needs form the basis for opportunities.

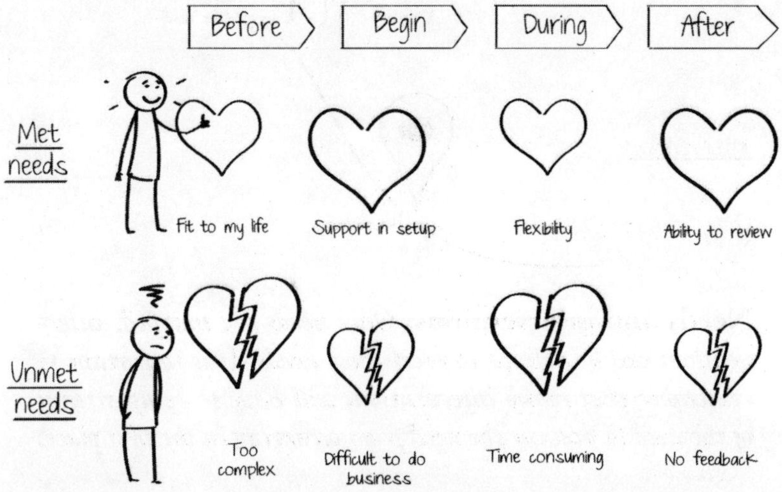

Met and unmet needs: *Simply mapping whether needs are met or not will help to highlight the areas of the service experience that need attention.*

2. **Developing concepts**

   Developing concepts can be surprisingly simple. It is about defining a way to meet unmet needs. However, it can be more complex, as it is rare that the need can be simply met by filling a gap. More often it is necessary for customers to take a different path through the experience from an earlier point in the journey. Think of it as an early intervention that meets a need downstream. If the need were not to fall off a cliff, the solution would be to warn people earlier not to catch them when they fall. To develop this kind of concept, find the best point to engage customers and take them on a better journey from there.

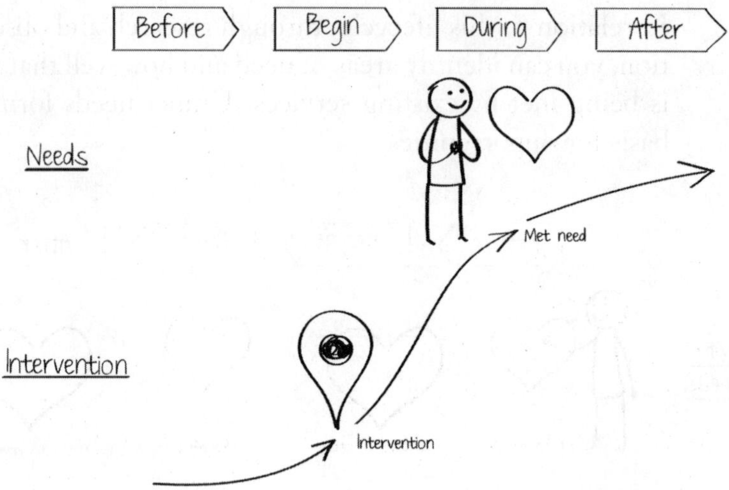

Needs and interventions: *Once needs are mapped, interventions can be defined to meet these needs. It is important to remember that many interventions will have to be up-stream of the need to prevent the need from occurring in the first place.*

How to Innovate Customer Propositions in Practice

A major retailer in a highly competitive sector identified a need to expand its innovation activities beyond the grocery market it was in. It felt that it had to do something radical to redefine its relationship with customers.

To do this, the company, working with Livework and other consultants, identified a number of life departments (travel, health, or career) that were high value to consumers and where there was a perceived innovation gap (a lack of breakthrough developments).

Once these life departments were agreed on, they were able to map the lifecycle of each department and understand how customers dealt with the challenges they faced by engaging customers for whom the life department was front of mind—those who had recently moved home, for example. This provided more detail as to where there was specific pain for the customers in the form of unmet needs. These needs were used as the basis for the definition of a range of opportunity areas that were prioritized and formed the basis for opportunities that were used to stimulate concept generation sessions across the business. With clear opportunities they were able to create a wide range of concepts by designing solutions for specific customer types. These concepts were developed and tested with customers to validate and refine before going into development and market beta.

These concepts entered a traditional innovation pipeline where they were evaluated for their business potential, development challenge, and consumer value. Through a number of cycles of design and testing with consumers, the ideas were rejected or refined toward a short list of high-potential options.

Takeaway Messages

1. To innovate requires stepping out of business as usual and into the customer context.
2. To understand the customers' context and get insight into unmet needs, we need to use higher-level human and consumer lifecycles.
3. For customer-driven innovation, identifying unmet needs is the basis for defining opportunities.

Chapter 4

Business Impact

Designing a Service around Customers' Needs Provides a New Way to Address Age-Old Business Challenges

Businesses have goals and challenges—growth and competition are two big examples. They generally employ the best tools they can find to achieve their goals and meet their challenges. Industry, technology, and markets evolve, and so do the tools required to operate. In a complex, networked, digital, and customer-driven world, service design can have impact on key business agenda.

Business impact is the ability to move forward—to understand a situation, develop solutions, and take them to market. Or is it the ability to adapt to new technologies and refine your ability to compete in a market? Often these situations involve customers—customers who must adopt, migrate, buy, use, or remain loyal to your business. With government services, impact is being able to have better results for less cost—these results are often outcomes for citizens in terms of health, well-being, and employment. Business impact regularly requires successful engagement of customers.

Thinking of business impact as being highly dependent of successful interactions and relationships with customers provides a new lens to tackle your challenges or strive for your goals. This lens is a way of seeing the business through the customers' eyes.

Service design provides an approach for understanding the business needs—it begins outside the business, in the markets, businesses, or lives of customers. This approach offers a fresh perspective on the challenges you face and new tools to address them.

This section of the book looks at four classic business challenges and illustrates how you can use a service design approach to address them. We explore how to innovate new business concepts, become more digital, achieve high customer performance and successfully launch new products or services.

INNOVATE NEW BUSINESS CONCEPTS

As markets change, businesses need to adapt. Different market factors such as competition, technology, or government policy can require a business to adapt. Conversely, most businesses are also on the lookout for new models that can give them an advantage in their market or help them enter new markets.

This need is not exclusive to commercial businesses. Government services need to innovate new ways to do their business that respond to demographic, political, or economic factors. We cannot continue to deliver services based on the models established in previous times.

Business concepts are necessary to provide a clear picture of *how we are going to do business* in the future. Developing business concepts is not unique to service design—far from it, it is the core of business strategy and marketing—service design offers a different approach that supports the creative process by making market insights, business concepts, and future scenarios more tangible.

> **INSIGHTS**
>
> Businesses are well practiced in understanding market trends but can get stuck between the insight and action as change is challenging. Finding ways to test and pilot new concepts through prototyping unlocks this by providing a way forward.

Why Read On?

- Understand how to identify and develop new business concepts.
- See how business concepts can give direction and purpose to the organization.
- Learn how to validate new concepts.

What Is a Business Concept?

A business concept is a clear idea of how to do business. A service design approach would add *how to do business with customers*. Ultimately, this is what business is—the model in which we bring value to customers. Innovating business concepts is different from innovating new customer propositions or experiences because the goal is to define a way the business works rather than something that it offers to customers.

Business concepts can be large and disruptive in their sector. A disruptive concept changes a sector, as the once original concept of a low-cost airline was to the stagnant air travel market, enabling new operators to enter the market. This concept was based on the insight that airlines were stuck in a model with high costs that could be removed, enabling operators to expand the addressable market.

Alternatively, a business concept can be differentiating for a company. A transformative concept is more about helping a company get out of a rut and responding to competition or taking a lead with a new idea. A good example of this is German kitchen appliance manufacturer Vorwerk, who sell their high-end food processer through a network of demonstrators, exploiting a direct and very different channel to market.

Business concepts have the value of being galvanizing for an organization. In both these cases the *big idea* enables the firm to have a very clear and precise understanding of their purpose and the *way they do business*.

How to Develop Business Concepts

Developing new concepts starts by identifying the need for a new way of doing business. Service design can help do so in three ways. The approach offers tools to collate pain points; it also provides methods to map customer and market trends onto lifecycles—and offers approaches to look at parallel models in different sectors. Service design also helps to validate new concepts by using scenarios and storytelling.

Business concepts start with clearly defined business problems. They may be a frustration with the complexity of the business or lack of direction or a specific pain point like customer churn or low margins. Identifying and naming these pains through internal discussions, or even work sessions that bring together a range of people from across the business, help to define the problem. Collating pain points from a number of people is likely to create patterns as different people bring up similar issues. These can be synthesized into a small number of core problems to address.

More-disruptive or opportunist business concepts can be initiated in a similar way but with less pain. Views on a market or a sector can be collated from experts and experienced professionals to create a similar assessment of the opportunity space. The people who started the first low-cost airlines would have seen how there was flab in the sector, unnecessary costs, and the opportunity to do things in a more lean fashion.

Unlike customer experience challenges, business concepts are more concerned with markets and customers en masse than customer needs. Feeding market and customer trends into your sector analysis helps to see the patterns and changes in your customer base or addressable market. What are the big trends in the market? What are customers doing differently compared to what they used to do? What are the trendsetting customers doing? What are influences of government policy changes?

For example, a business-to-business service mapped the market to its lifecycle and broke down the market by size of company. They found that while the larger companies were staying loyal and using their service effectively, smaller businesses were resigning their accounts with much higher frequency. This led them to investigate new ways of doing business with smaller firms and explore new pricing models and terms of agreement that would work for this section of the market.

Understanding the actors and factors influencing customers from the outside in enables us to get a better handle on what is going on in the market. Actors are the other people or organizations that customers interact with. It could be other customers' businesses that are setting a new example of how to do business or individuals such as family dynamics and how they are changing. Factors are more abstract influences such as government policy, economic conditions, or changing social norms.

To ground these actors and factors, they can be related to the customer or consumer lifecycle by asking how they influence customer behavior and where in the cycle. Do they influence the size of the addressable market that could be made a new offer or do they change the nature of the way existing customers can be served? Often a business concept is about being different in a market, so it is likely to reflect on how you think about the early stages of a lifecycle, *before* people become customers. But it can influence how you *begin* the relationship or what you do with existing customers *during* their experience as customers to retain, cross-sell, or migrate them to new ways of doing business. An example of this would be a technology firm that has a new way of delivering their software and needs to migrate customers from an older version or platform.

To do this you need to be able to quantify these trends and pinpoint the stage in the lifecycle where changing actors and factors are having an influence. This could be by plotting where in a lifecycle a new regulation affects your customers and how that impacts your business. If this new regulation requires more thorough checks on new customers then it impacts the setup or onboarding stage of the cycle and could reduce the number of active customers unless you find a different way of doing business around this registration point. The key benefit of doing analysis this way is it provides a visual representation of how these factors are affecting business in relation to the lifecycle. Visually representing things like reduced customer activation or higher churn makes the impact more tangible—a call to action.

Business concepts can often be out there ready to be discovered. There are a finite number of business models, and most have been thought of; however, surprisingly few companies look outside their sector for inspiration. Simply looking for parallel industry cases can provide a range of business concepts that you can try on for size. To do this, describe what you would like customers to be doing and then develop ideas for how to incentivize them to do what you desire.

Many will fail but some will bring insight and spark new ideas. The trick is to find cases where there is a parallel—not simply a parallel industry, but a parallel problem or opportunity. Surgical teams can learn from racing car pit stops. Think about the challenge you have and who has a similar challenge that you can learn from. Live-work once used nightclubs as an example for how a media company could rethink its subscription services.

Once you have identified your concept options, either by collating pain points, mapping market and customer trends, or looking outside your sector, they need to be validated. To do this, your emerging business concepts should be translated into stories or scenarios that can be used to engage stakeholders and customers for feedback and evaluation.

A business concept may be something like: *we should think of ourselves as a club!* A story or scenario would describe what that club is like. How do people hear about it, what is the joining process, who can join, what do you get as a member? Telling this story will help you bring the concept to life and test it in more detail. This will help you to hone in on the concept that has the most impact. The extent of this testing can vary hugely, depending on the situation, risk, and complexity of development. Testing should progress through levels of fidelity, from quick and dirty to full pilot.

Although concepts require testing and development, in their essence they can be valid and provide value. Do not wait for full proof before using your concept to reenergize the organization. A concept can provide a direction before the detail is fully understood. It can be right in principle, and that principle can guide you forward toward the goal. The concept should be flexible enough for interpretation in development but simple enough to act as an elevator pitch to explain and enthuse.

Approaches to Developing Business Concepts

1. **Mapping actors and factors**

   Mapping actors and factors to the lifecycle can give you a picture of how these things relate to your business or sector. Where are these actors and factors influencing you? Is it *before* in relation to your offer or during in relation to your customer base?

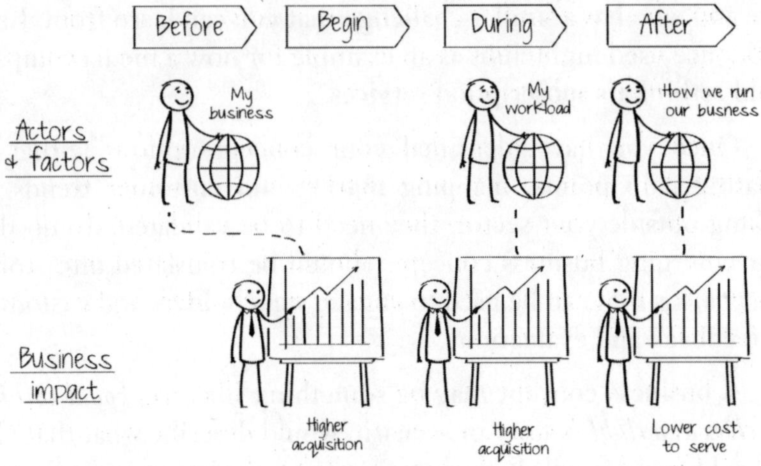

Actors and factors: *Pinpointing where an actor or factor impacts the lifecycle helps to see the business impact.*

2. **Testing concepts using business scenarios**

   When exploring different concepts, perhaps concepts borrowed from parallel industries, it can help to see these as scenarios that you can describe as a story in relation to your customer or consumer lifecycle. Take the concept and draw it out as a story about how you are doing business with customers at key stages.

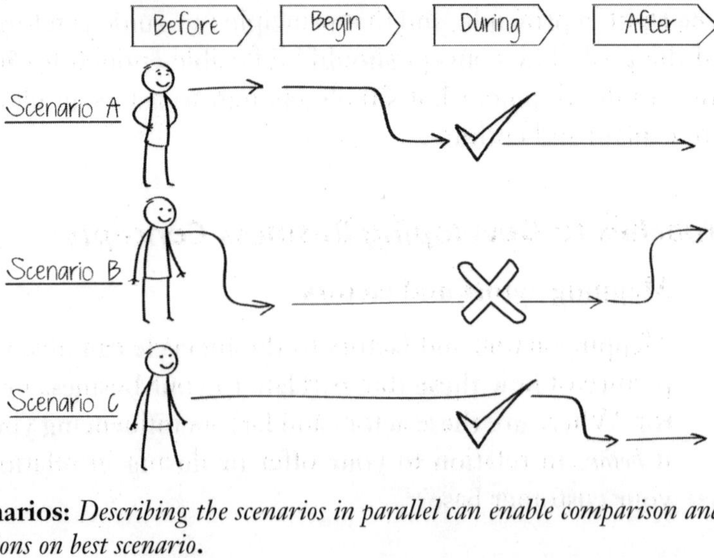

Scenarios: *Describing the scenarios in parallel can enable comparison and decisions on best scenario.*

Solving a Business Issue with a New Business Concept

A midsize telematics company that provided security devices and services for luxury cars found its market changing. It had grown on the back of insurance mandates for additional security on expensive cars, but this requirement was declining, leading to fewer sales, while on the other end customers were retiring their contracts in increasing volumes.

The firm needed to respond to these challenges to attract new customers and retain existing ones.

On investigation it became clear that the model they had in place, built around the requirement for the device to be installed on the cars, had the firm stuck in a product concept that was no longer relevant. This approach had left them without a clear purpose or idea of how they should do business in a proactive manner.

Taking a customer perspective, we discovered how customers did not value a box installed in their car that in an ideal world they would never have need of. We also looked into parallel services and saw that in B2B telematics a very different model was in use. B2B users were not sold a box but offered a service package that enabled them to monitor their fleets. The box was simply an enabler.

From these insights we explored options for how to think of the box as an enabler rather than the core proposition. The firm needed to define a new way that they did business with customers. They knew from firsthand research that customers still valued the peace of mind that the box represented, but that was not what they were being sold.

Looking at other services in other sectors, but related to risk, insurance, and peace of mind, we noticed that breakdown organizations like the AA in the United Kingdom sell membership rather than a product. Membership entitles customers to a range of benefits but also enrolls them in a club that does more than simply pick them up when they break down.

Membership became the proposed business concept for the telematics firm. While developing the concept, a shift took place in the way the team members thought about their business and their relationship with customers. Membership gave them a reason to talk to customers about other things aside from renewing their contract. They could provide additional services such as airport monitoring of your car and had a reason to interact with members about security in general.

Armed with this new concept, the business was able to address its retention and customer engagement challenges.

Takeaway Messages

1. New business concepts enable organizations to have a clear and precise understanding of their purpose and the *way they do business.*
2. Identifying new concept options can be done by collating pain points, mapping market and customer trends onto lifecycles, or looking outside your sector.
3. Scenarios and storytelling are useful tools to discover the concepts that will have the largest impact.
4. Concepts should be flexible enough for interpretation in development and simple enough to act as an elevator pitch to explain and enthuse the organization.

BECOMING A *MORE* DIGITAL BUSINESS

Digital first is a major buzzword—and it's what many customers expect. Digital technologies promise greater efficiencies and—depending on your perspective—present a major opportunity or pressure to catch up.

Although seemingly easy for start-ups, digital poses a much more complex challenge than it should for established large businesses and for government. The process of shifting service delivery to a new digital channel can cause huge uncertainty, confusion, and mess. Digital collapses traditional boundaries—between departments, intermediaries, or organizations—and challenges

established safe processes and practices. A shift to digital is not simply a channel shift; it is a different way of doing business. This adds to the complexity and the challenge. In addition, the transition to digital threatens established roles, jobs, and expertise. Finally, although a future digital business is relatively easy to conceive, the transition from "as is" to "to be" is far more complex and challenging.

Service design offers a different take on the challenge of digital. Rather than focus on digital in and of itself, the approach looks at digital as just another—if particularly powerful and disruptive—way to meet customer needs. The customer lens provides a way to put digital options in context and make better decisions. A service design approach ensures that digital initiatives achieve two things: value to customers by reducing waste and complexity, and quicker, easier, and more direct interactions between customers and services.

INSIGHTS

- Taking a customer-needs driven approach as the basis for digital developments provides a unique opportunity to reduce complexity in your services. Taking out activities that slow down the customer will provide the efficiencies that digital promised.
- Building capability requirements on the back of customer needs will clarify what is important for your digital service model. Having this clarity will enable clear assessment of your current processes and enable assessment of existing or proposed systems.
- Adopting a migration strategy based on offering customers new digital services when they are engaged with your business exploits the opportunity to renew and improve relationships. If customers see that you have developed alternative and valuable new ways to achieve their needs when they are paying attention, they will appreciate it.

Why Read On?

- See how to put digital options in the context of customer needs.
- Understand how to transition customers to digital channels.
- Learn how to move toward a desired future digital model.

What Is a Digital Business?

Despite all the *Wired* magazine–style noise about digital revolution, generally digital simply enables customers to do what they did before but faster, with more control or with better information to guide their choices. The revolution is in business, where established models are challenged and disrupted. The trouble for established businesses is that it also opens the door for new, smarter, and faster competition to disrupt their market by achieving these customer benefits before they are able to make the shift themselves. This is why once a business sets a digital strategy, it is desperate to achieve the transformation yesterday. There are numerous examples of how industries have been disrupted by digital from retail led by Amazon to the potential that Tele-care offers the health sector.

Digital presents a huge opportunity, and there is pressure to make the transition—but nobody is really clear about what to transform to, what needs to change, and how to get there. What are the logical steps?

When looking at future digital scenarios from inside a large organization, the danger is to replicate the existing situation with existing process and relationships. The trouble is that this will create hugely complex digital experiences for customers. Understanding the customer's view of the service and your organization will help develop simple digital experiences.

Ultimately what businesses need to do is identify the digital capabilities that will enhance their performance and customers' satisfaction.

How to Guide a Digital Strategy

The only way to ensure that the transformation to digital seizes the efficiency and customer experience gains that it has promised is to design your future digital services from the customer perspective. The outside-in view starts with understanding customer needs and defining your future or "target" customer experience based on these needs, not your business processes.

With digital challenges it is important to identify which customer needs can be met with digital means. Many needs for information and transactions can be met digitally, as the technologies are well suited for this. Customers will, however, still need to interact with you in ways that may require human support. The goal is to be able to use your people to meet the high-level needs that require human advice and guidance and to free them up to do so by removing the more mundane transactional tasks from their workload.

This approach will provide a scenario that may appear impossible—if we are true to customer needs and the benefits of digital then we should be cutting out a number of things that cause customer frustration. This can include delays in simple processes such as setting up an account or registering an issue, providing customers with information or data that they previously could not access or giving them direct control over their contract, enabling greater flexibility.

A service design approach always starts with clearly defined customer needs and outcomes. Insight into customer needs comes from two rich sources: customers and the people they engage with on the frontline. Customer needs can be understood from their behaviors and experiences. To gain this insight, a range of approaches can be taken, from shadowing customers in different aspects of the experience and discussing past experiences with them. This provides insight into attitudes and mind-sets.

What customers say and what they do is often different, so analyzing customer behavior data is a great complement to firsthand observations. This data could be complaints logs, activity volumes around specific tasks, and analysis of business volume at different times of day or year. Equally valuable is to understand what customer-related activity employees are executing and the effort required. How much staff time is adding value for customers? Understanding these tasks can often lead directly to insight into needs that could be met with digital means.

Understanding and mapping these insights to customer lifecycles and journeys provide the customer requirements that enable you to define a target customer experience. This target will state what customers should be able to achieve at each stage of the journey and the outcomes and benefits of their being able to do so. From this, you will be able to define what a digital platform can do to deliver this experience. It is important to think of digital first as the capability to deliver information, interactions, and transactions to customers directly. Only then should you think of the digital channel (web, app, mobile, etc.) that this capability is delivered through. This enables greater flexibility and future proofing.

A target customer experience provides a context to evaluate capabilities – to find out if they are present in the organization – or to understand if they would be challenging to develop or buy. Separating these capabilities from customer needs is essential, as this enables an ongoing gap analysis between the target experience and the experience that can be delivered at a given point in development or transition.

Capabilities also have the benefit of being neutral to specific technologies and systems. They should provide a set of requirements against which to evaluate possible solutions or systems. A capability also crosses functional areas so an assessment can be made of what is required of sales and service departments to deliver a business capability.

Think of the approach as being an ongoing dialogue between customer needs and business capabilities. "Can we meet this need?" "Yes, if we develop this capability!"

Once you are clear on customer needs and have defined a target experience, you may find that there is a gap between this vision and what feels feasible in your organization. A faster account opening process will seem impossible with existing processes and systems (let alone legal restrictions). It is important to realize that this gap exists and to not water down the target customer experience but to manage the transformation toward that target, knowing that it is not going to happen overnight. To do this, it helps to translate the customer needs and the target experience into capabilities that your business needs to develop. These capabilities can be aligned to business benefits and outcomes.

Armed with a set of target experiences, an understanding of the capabilities required, and an idea of the potential benefits, you can begin a process of prioritization and planning based on a balanced evaluation of the level of customer need, business benefit, and organizational feasibility.

Many businesses are concerned about the transition from a current situation—where customers do business with them over the phone, face-to-face, or even through the mail—to the future situation, where digital is the default channel. They are often concerned about either building new digital capabilities but having to maintain the other channels, too, to serve customers who prefer or are attached to these channels, or they are worried that they will have to "turn off" these channels and force customers to digital, damaging customer relationships.

The best approach to this is to design a migration journey that recognizes that the customers have to move and identify the best points for their transitions. This journey must start with clarity about who the customers are and their current situation. This can be simple things like "Are they existing or new customers, frequent or infrequent, digitally savvy or not?" Different journeys may be required for different customer types, and journeys can be prioritized based on the desired adoption patterns across the customer base. What is needed is a middle state, an "*a to b*" design.

What is missing from these scenarios—and from most thinking about digital business—is the recognition that digital is a channel alongside other channels. A design is required for how the channels will work together with each other but also how to actively migrate customers from existing channels to digital ones.

Take a transport metaphor: journeys are made up of both the mode of transport (car, train, and plane) and the interfaces between these modes (stations, parking, interchanges). We need to design interchanges between channels that migrate customers to digital at times in their journey where it makes sense for them to do so. This will generally be when the customer is engaged in something that matters to them, when they start a new or renewed contract, when they are resolving an issue, or when they are experiencing a change in their personal or business circumstances. At these points they need help and are receptive to listen to new ways of doing business together.

Apply this metaphor to digital within a wider service or customer experience and you see how it is necessary to think of how customers are introduced to new digital capabilities. A customer who is accustomed to doing business on the phone cannot simply be directed to the new online facility. They need to be introduced to it in a way that explains the benefits and features. The same applies to customers who are interacting digitally but have a need for human support for advice. Connecting them to this in a way that enables the agent to take over where the digital experience left off makes for a much better experience and a more effective interaction.

In practice, everything is a bit messier than the theory described above. Changes have unforeseen, as well as hoped for, impacts on customers and the business, and it is essential to check in on both the target experience and the required capabilities at regular intervals. A change that enables customers to do something new can have an impact on priorities and plans, and the process should be flexible enough to change direction between iterations or releases if required. Feedback from customers and staff and against performance indicators should be built into the launch and release planning with the opportunity to check on impact and refine activities in light of feedback. Expected benefits should be tracked and analyzed in detail. Sometimes a customer journey throws up unseen barriers that are only visible in a real operating context. Cycles of prototypes and early-stage launches with smaller customer numbers can mitigate these issues but in life improvement is essential.

Approaches to Using Scenarios for Becoming Digital

1. **Align digital to evergreen customer needs**

   Digital features should be designed to respond to customer needs rather than what is possible. This helps to keep digital services lean and simple for customers. Align different digital channels to enable a seamless integrated experience.

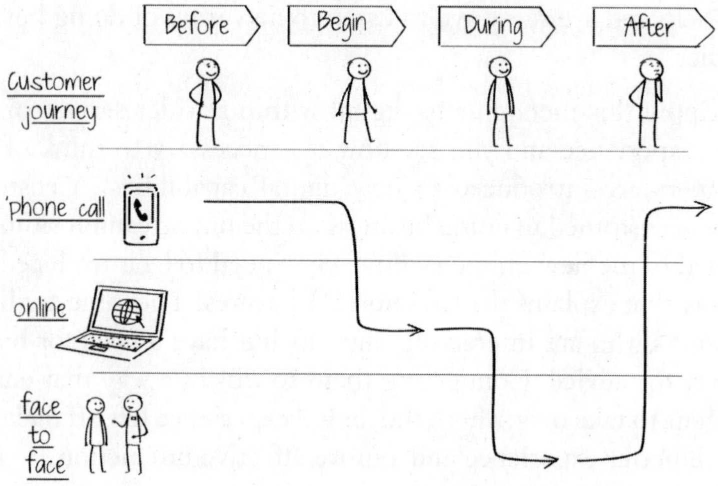

Channels: *Aligning channels to the stages and phases of a lifecycle or customer journey enables you to see how they can connect and interoperate.*

2. **Design to migrate customers**

   We can design customer journeys that deliberately migrate customers to digital channels by defining the right moment to introduce customers to the digital capability. These should be moments when you have the customers' attention and ability to channel shift.

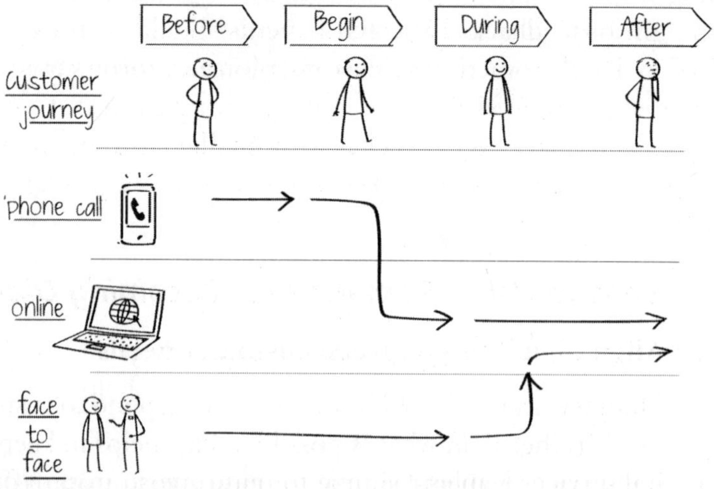

Migration: *Using the multichannel view, you can then plan customer pathways that support business goals such as channel migration.*

How to Develop a Digital Business in Practice

A large financial services firm found itself behind the curve with digital. They had invested in a haphazard manner in local initiatives, not realizing that digital needed to be a core competence.

Government changes pushing for greater consumer choice and transparency meant that it needed to be much better at interacting directly with customers to retain them through key transitions (such as from pension to annuity). Also, competitors moved more quickly, and the firm found themselves needing to develop digital solutions quickly.

Due to this pressure, it needed to make sure that it focused on doing the things that really mattered, not every concept could be developed in digital. The only way to do this was to understand what customers really needed in the specific transitions in each customer journey. The team focused on the key transition points from one life stage to another (and one financial product to another) and on how they could support customers through these changes.

The information, interaction, transaction model came into play as the firm saw that many customers found the sector and products confusing and choices difficult. These needs could be supported by impartial information with the benefit that customers favored the company that they found the clearest and tended to stay with that company for their purchases.

Second, the company realized that it thinks of products to be sold (financial products like funds, pensions, etc.). However, customers have choices to make and the products come at the end of making the choice. The firm discovered that it could not simply think of selling this product with a big **buy** button. You must support the customer decision making and choice through more subtle **interactions** with consultative tools or human advice and guidance. Breaking this choice down into a journey in itself helped to detail these specific transactions.

This approach enables the firm to build a road map of digital features that they could start work on immediately and see results in customer behavior and satisfaction as early as possible.

Takeaway Messages

1. It is important to think of digital first as the capability to deliver information, interactions, and transactions to customers directly.
2. Translate the customer needs and the target experience into capabilities that your business needs to develop.

ACHIEVE HIGHER CUSTOMER PERFORMANCE

To deliver successful service, businesses, organizations, and customers need to perform well. Businesses and government bodies want customers or service users to behave in certain ways. They want customers to do simple things like buy products and services, but also to use their services efficiently and effectively to ensure that they get the value they were looking for. Services can be designed in a way that inspires certain behavior and performance by customers, enabling the smooth running of a service.

Customer performance is a critical factor in successful outcomes in every service industry. And successful outcomes are needed to run a sustainable business. Guiding customer performance is often highly desired in business but addressing it is less well understood. A service design approach puts customer performance at the forefront and offers methods to design the service in a way that puts you in greater control. To do this we can look at what services need to do to inspire, enable, and support customers to behave in ways that deliver positive outcomes—for themselves, business, or society.

> **INSIGHTS**
>
> - The idea of customer performance can be quite foreign to many businesses. It really does help to take people out to meet and more importantly observe customer behaviors to help them see how customers behave.
> - The idea of supporting customers to behave differently can seem overwhelming, as it implies major efforts—it can be useful to think of the smallest new behavior that has an impact and build from there.

Why Read On?

- Understand how services are co-produced by businesses and customers.
- See how to design for high-performing customers.
- Understand the role of service provider as a platform for behavior.

What Is Customer Performance?

Organizations generally refer to performance as the undertaking of specified or unspecified activities by people, processes, and systems. People delivering a service have performance targets and quality controls. The outcome of performance is expected to create measurable value.

Customer performance is rarely as well defined or governed by contracts. Generally customers cannot be tied to agreements as to what they must or must not do. However, as services get more effective in their own operations, they are looking to the next challenge: getting customers to contribute to greater success.

Several examples help to explore where and when customer performance is key to success. One area is when there is a high volume of customers using a service, such as with public transport or a sporting event. Here customers need to perform their bit to ensure safety and security, but also to make the experience better by providing the right atmosphere either on a train or in a stadium. Service providers aim to influence these behaviors for the good of the service to all customers. A great example is the famous "stand on the right on the escalator" and "mind the gap" announcements on London Underground that increase safety and mobility in stations.

Another London example is from the 2012 Olympics, where customers were educated about minor sports before events to help them be better-informed spectators and improve the atmosphere in the arena.

It is important to understand that key performance measures such as acquiring, activating, and retaining customers all require customer performance as well as business performance. Customers must do things to complete these transactions—even simple tasks like inputting their personal data—and their ability to do their tasks efficiently and effectively has an impact on business success. Seeing the customer as an active agent rather than as a passive consumer is key to successfully supporting customer performance.

Customers also play a key role in managing cost to serve. Customers have to perform in basic business activities such as sales, where customers must often provide information about their specific needs. When a sale is a complex one, this customer task can be much bigger than we recognize—think of the procurement of equipment or software for a business and how much effort customers must make to decide on what is best for them. Once a sale is made many businesses still need customers to be active users of their services for the service to be received and valued. Inactive customers are not likely to renew or buy more. Take a service or product like software, where a customer must not simply buy but also install, set up, roll out, and train users.

The more we ask of customers—in terms of self-service, adoption of new and more efficient technologies or within complex systems—the more customer performance can be the critical factor in the success or failure of a service. At a time where businesses are looking for a new competitive edge, your customer could be the solution.

How to Approach Customer Performance

Customers cannot generally be managed to perform in a certain way. At each stage of their lifecycle as customers, people may need to be *inspired* or motivated to continue to use the service. At almost every step, the service must *enable* them to achieve their goals and complete specific tasks. Finally, at key points they may need *support* from experts.

Let's look at the performance of a purchase to illustrate this model and demonstrate the effect of customer performance. It is easy to see how the first part of the model relates to a purchase: customers must be motivated, or *inspired*. The world of advertising is well aware of this and has honed methods to inspire people to engage in considering a purchase. In sales it is important to identify customer motivations and work with them to gain their commitment and investment in the process. Customers also need to be enabled to make a purchase, they need the right technologies, and they need to know how to use them. This may seem obvious but every new payment technology requires customers to be trained to use it before it becomes fully adopted. Finally, customers often need *support* in a purchase, especially if the product or service is complex. They may need advice on making a choice of how the product will fit into their needs. Think about choosing an expensive wine in a restaurant to go with your meal.

Many selling approaches start with the business and what it has and needs to sell. Service design approaches sales from the customer perspective, exploring what they need in order to be able to buy. This enables a business to understand the actors and factors that influence a customer's decision making and design an approach that meets these needs.

A service design approach helps to structure the customer experience through the lifecycle and specific customer journeys, and helps to pinpoint the moments in each stage of the service that customers need inspiration, enabling, or support. From this baseline understanding we can create future scenarios that describe how the customer could be inspired, enabled, and supported. Then we can work out how we deliver these requirements in ways that will improve their performance.

Before, Begin, During, and After

The four stages of the customer experience—before, begin, during, and after—can be used to identify when customers need to be inspired, supported, or enabled.

Before customers buy or use a service, they may need training or preparation. Preparation means understanding options and deciding on their course of action. This could apply to planning travel, moving home, or installing software. The customer has a job to be done and needs to decide on how to do it. Spending time with customers with a focus on the question "What is the job they are undertaking?" will give you a clearer understanding and a context for your services as you learn how your service fits their priorities. This is important for service providers to understand, as often they see customers as passive consumers rather than people involved in achieving a goal that they may need support with. Helping the customers in their planning is adding value. The business benefit of doing so can be that it grows sales, or grows the market. Customers will need a mix of *inspiration*, *enabling* technologies and *support* to develop their game plan. Without it they cannot move forward.

The *beginning* of a customer's engagement with a service is a critical point. We often talk about a "perfect start" of a customer relationship. Getting the start right affects the whole experience that follows. There are a number of truths that we can apply here that give us a start. Customers generally understand the contract they have less well than we assume they do. It is good to plan for how they are *set up* for the new relationship rather than dropping them in as if they are seasoned customers. Customer also will have a *first-use* experience, and it is important to think of this as different to subsequent uses. It is where they familiarize and explore (or don't). Designing a specific *first-use* experience helps enormously. Think of the first time you drive a new model of car and the acclimatization required and apply that feeling to your service.

This recognizes that customers' needs for support at the beginning are different. Setting a customer up well means that they are more likely to use a service as it was intended, and play their role. A poor setup can lead to customers coming back for changes or queries that do not add value and add cost to serve. This principle applies to the good setup of a customer with a new mortgage as well as a patient coming to terms with a diagnosis of illness that requires them to perform things that keep them well (change diet, take medication). Often investment in the *beginning* pays off later in the service in reduced costs and better outcomes for customers (leading to happy customers or better-off patients). Simply understanding where the customers are starting from, their level of knowledge, confidence, or time available, can help you design a setup that really works.

During a service explores when and how a service enables customers to perform. To be successful, a service needs to stick to the plan and remind customers of that plan and always be ready to respond to needs and changes as they occur. A good service will remind players of their individual roles in the performance and also adjust tactics to respond to events. You may find out that a good way to remind your customers of their role is to schedule regular updates. One cable company in the United Kingdom enables its customers to get the most from its set-top box through an email newsletter. Second, it can be done as a response to customer requests. Be ready to help customers resolve issues that are predictable. You can define these predictable needs through analysis of behavioral data, complaints, or bottlenecks in the flow of a service. Timing is critical here, and this is when a more detailed understanding of a customer's journey through the lifecycle pays off. Pay attention to how customers progress through the service, what steps they take from first use to regular use, how they get to become better performers, and what they need to get there. Notice the timing of this journey and design interventions that support customers at each step.

A great example of this was a service designed to enable patients through a challenging medical treatment. We could predict the challenges patients would face from interview and historical data and design interventions for key stages in the treatment to support them with needs around work, family, or fatigue needs.

Sticking to the plan requires reminding customers of how things work and what they need to do, just as the London Underground continues to remind us to "mind the gap." This is, however, not enough because the service as enabler must also push customers toward higher levels of performance by changing their game plan. London Underground is doing this right now by coaching regular passengers to use new contactless payment options. You do this with a mix of *inspiration* and *enablement*, excite customers about new options, and make it easier for them to adopt them.

Finally, it is important to consider what customers need and where there is value *after* a service is finished. With services that are repeated on a regular basis, this is critical. Imagine the insurance service that works with you to be more secure on a regular basis by reviewing the risks and how you can help to mitigate them. Can you get customers to reflect on their performance and perform better next time? This can be done by designing the service in a way that customers feel it is working with them to achieve a shared goal—*let us get you more secure!* Define the goal and design interactions with the customers, which encourage them to do more by suggesting things they can do to improve performance.

Some car insurance services are starting to use telematics to support customers to become safer drivers by providing them with performance feedback.

Approaches to Enabling Better Customer Performance

1. **Specifying high-performing services**

   The desire for high-performing customers is driven by business goals. One of these goals may be for satisfied customers, but harder goals are more important. These goals should be mapped and understood before designing a customer approach.

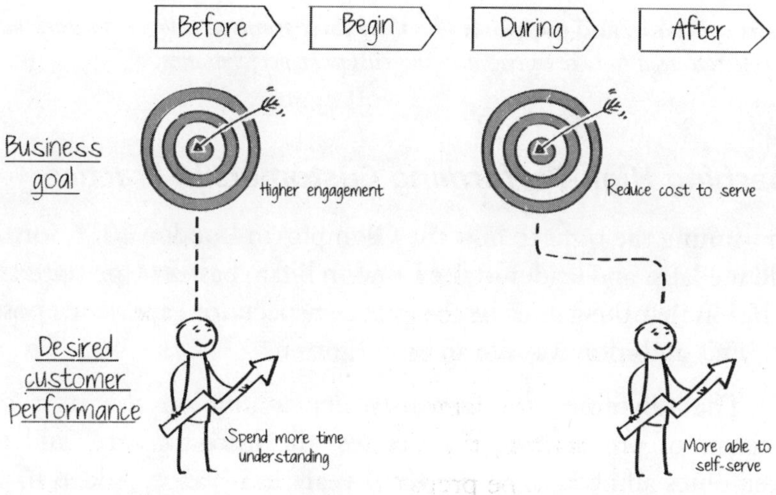

Customer performance: *Know the business goal at each stage of a customer journey, and then work out how customer performance can support this goal.*

2. **Designing for high-performing customers**

   Now that we know the business goal and the desired customer performance, we can develop an approach to deliver them. Understand the opportunities to inspire, enable, and support customers at each stage of the service. As always, these options must be based on strong insight into customer needs but also driven by the business goals for each stage.

Inspire, enable and support: *Use these three words as triggers to work out the role you need to take in encouraging customer performance.*

Coaching High-Performing Customers in Practice

On winning the right to host the Olympics in London 2012, former gold medalist and leader of the London bid Sebastian Coe stated his ambition that the games be the greatest spectator experience possible. This ambition was not to be forgotten.

The Olympics are famously demanding on the host city in terms of preparation, the venues, the infrastructure, and the ceremonies all need to be prepared years in advance. Added to the many teams preparing for the event was the first ever spectator experience team in Olympic history. With the level of attention on the games and the strategy in London to use existing and sometimes old venues, the team focused on the risks involved as much as the needs of spectators. Risks such as people being late or venues overcrowding were high on the register for the games management team.

Armed with previous experience and an analysis of what made the best visitor experiences of other events great, the team members identified two aspects of a great spectator experience. The first was something that you would expect from a global sporting event, what they called magic moments. These were the highlights that spectators might expect—live experience of athletic achievement, drama, and competition. The second aspect they realized that they needed to deliver was more prosaic, but essential: the team members called it brilliant basics. They realized that many little things could mar or even ruin a once-in-a-lifetime experience. Brilliant basics would mean that spectators got to where they needed to be on time, refreshed, comfortable, and ready for the magic. And got home smoothly, too.

Moving thousands of spectators around many venues across a city like London and into their seats on time is a major operation. The Olympic team members realized that two challenges could be addressed at once—a great spectator experience and smooth, safe, and timely circulation of people. They needed high-performing spectators. To do this they needed to inspire, enable, and support all visitors.

They used different tools to inspire customer performance. For example, they knew from people who had worked on previous Olympics that minority sports had an issue with audiences who didn't understand the rules and therefore didn't have the optimal experience. To address this the designed exhibitions in the waiting areas before events explained the rules and dynamics of the sports. This meant that when customer entered the arena they were better, more engaged spectators, enjoyed the event more, and looked better on TV.

The key thing spectators needed was to be enabled to navigate their way to the right seat in the right venue at the right time. The team members discovered this through working with crowd management experts, venue management, and discussing the experience people had with previous games. They developed ways to understand and map the journeys spectators would need to take and anticipate issues they would encounter. They then designed interventions to counter these issues or prepare spectators for them (such as a long walk once at a venue). This began the day they received their tickets and critically the time that they planned to set off for the games. The games organizers were aware of the time it could take to get to and through the venues to the seats but most spectators were not. If they left home too late, they could miss the performance or cause trouble by rushing and not engaging in the other offers of a day at the games. Ticket reminder communications were designed to give customers a clear countdown to enable them to plan their travel and arrive on good time in good shape.

Finally, when at the games spectators needed clear support to stay on plan. The Olympic team devised perhaps the most memorable aspect of the games (outside the sports themselves): the games makers. Games makers were volunteers who populated all the venues supporting spectators to perform their bit in a great spectator experience, as well as safe and successful navigation of venues. Games makers both helped visitors find their way around and find the amenities they needed but also provided motivation to the spirits of spectators at key points such as queues and crowded areas through enthusiasm. The games team designed on-site entertainment, such as music and street theater, to support crowd flows. This could be used to hold people back or move people on, depending on the needs—and do so without spoiling the spectator experience.

The London Olympics was heralded as a great experience and an achievement for the city. The games makers and the spectators were understood to be an inherent part of this success and the feeling that the Olympics belonged to the people.

Takeaway Messages

1. Businesses and customers need to perform well for a service to be a success.
2. Think of a service as an enabler of customer performance.
3. Define the business goals and desired customer performance first.
4. Identify when and how to inspire, enable, and support customers to help them perform their part in the performance.

SUCCESSFUL LAUNCH AND ADOPTION OF A NEW PRODUCT OR SERVICE

The decision to develop a new proposition may be driven by a new emerging technology, by the potential to leverage a unique capability, or even as a defensive move to fend off a competitor. Whatever the motivation, the launch of a new offer can have serious risks attached. A core risk is that the proposition will promise a lot and then not deliver. Often there is a risk that customers fail to get value from something new, not because it isn't a good offer but that a supporting aspect of the service fails. They cannot set it up well or integrate it into their world.

A service design approach will help you to avoid a number of pitfalls that might impede your new service from being a success. It does this by ensuring that a customer view is included in the preparations and design before launch, and those aspects of the experience are tested and validated before the costs of launch have occurred. Most important of all, this approach can help you focus on what will compel customers to embrace your new offering for it to take off in the market.

INSIGHTS

- When development teams don't integrate a strong customer focus early in the process, they often end up marred with customer faults that are hard to improve due to technical or organizational constraints.
- Designing the before—and after—experience is as important as designing the launch experience itself.
- Simulating launch experiences with customers is critical to success and can be conducted quickly, cheaply, and in quick iterations until you achieve certainty that the experience is right.

Why Read On?

- Discover how you can avoid the pitfalls of launching a new product or service.
- Identify critical success factors for success with customers in a systematic way.
- Learn how to design a customer adoption journey.

Successful Launches and Adoption Journeys

When a company decides to take a new proposition to market, it helps to differentiate between launch and adoption. A company may develop a brilliantly conceived proposition and successfully launch it but fail to gain return on investment if customers don't adopt it as part of their everyday habits. For example, a million customers may enthusiastically download an innovative payment app, but if they still prefer using their plastic card the entire investment will be lost.

A successful launch requires giving customers a clear, up-front view of the benefits the new product or service will actually bring them. A TV provider offering a new channel package will need to communicate this in different ways than a hospital offering a new type of surgery. In any case, changing behavior will meet resistance from both customers and staff—that's why it is important to carefully design for this resistance.

Gaining a precise understanding of a customer's decision points creates most value for the business. It might be easy to assume that people who need, want, or desire a service will automatically become customers. But in reality, a number of small things like faulty web forms, payment issues, or waiting too long to get a confirmation can prompt customers to reject an offer they've already mentally accepted. This is why you must design for an experience that guides potential customers all the way through the process and familiarizes them with the new offer. This will avoid the likelihood that they'll drop off.

Many businesses also fail to acknowledge how important the experience of first use is to customers. In some cases, up to one-third of new customers reject the service if they cannot get it to work as expected on the first try. New concepts that require customers to adopt a new behavior have a bigger challenge than established or "me too" offers. If you design a perfect start for customers—during the first minutes, days, and weeks of the engagement (adoption)—they are likely to reward you with loyalty and additional purchases.

How to Design a Successful Launch and Adoption Journey

Service design can help to design a strong launch strategy, and more importantly, it will help to design an experience that encourages customers to engage and adopt the service beyond first-time use and grow usage over time. Businesses that carefully design for the customer experience before, during, and after the launch of a new process, product, or service are more likely to "get it right" from day one.

Approaching launch and adoption from a customer perspective starts with gaining a clear view of the *actors* and *factors* that influence customers' perceptions and decisions. For example, a factor such as access to TV over broadband Internet will influence the behavior of cable TV customers infinitely more than a new, attractive, and well-priced channel package. An actor such as Spotify has massively disrupted the "product model" in the music industry, laying the ground for a whole new set of businesses to enter (and leave) the market. Actors and factors outside of the company's control will usually influence customers' expectations and experience more than any service provider will be able to on their own. Therefore, it is extremely important to build outside-in understanding of the context that customers experience before you design the launch strategy for a new service.

Using consumer lifecycles to map the influence of actors and factors through different phases is a practical way to get started with a systematic approach to design a relevant launch experience for customers. The consumer lifecycle typically describes consumer behavior in the main phases and stages of their relationship with a sector and industry over a four- to eight-year cycle. For example, it can describe typical buying, using, and defection behavior of cell phone customers, and their general experience of the telecoms industry. When you analyze the actors and factors that affect people's behaviors with an industry, you gain a powerful view of customers' expectations to your proposition and how they are likely to compare it to their current experience.

The next step is to build on the consumer lifecycle and design a "customer adoption journey," detailing the desired experience from first awareness of the proposition to a steady, sustainable relationship with the service. The key to the adoption journey is to identify exactly where customers make decisions to try, buy, and use the service, and design the ideal experience to move them along the journey toward loyal customers. Avoid making compromises on features that enable customers to decide to move on, as they will end up having a directly negative effect on the bottom line. For example, in the payment app example, any investment will be worth it to move people from just downloading the app to making the first mobile purchase.

The key to an adoption journey is to recognize that this is the first time for customers. It may be the first time they have tried something like this, the first time they have bought it in a specific way, or the first time they have used it. When designing one of the first car clubs in Europe, we realized that a visual step-by-step description of how to use the car for the first time would increase adoption. Through the entire joining journey we repeatedly reinforced this message. As a result, customers knew what to expect, and found it easy to use the cars at their first try.

Approaches to Designing the Adoption Journey

1. **Describe the decision-making journeys**

   Different customers behave differently. Map the adoption journeys for 80 percent of your customers to gain a clear picture of where you should invest in the customer experience to gain return on your investment.

Adoption needs: *Designing for the first test, purchase, and setup will enable a stronger adoption journey.*

2. **Identify customer barriers and opportunities before, during, and after the decision**

   Use existing data about similar services to pinpoint where potential customers may stumble into the adoption and usage process. Supplement with qualitative research and interviews with a small number of customers and customer-facing staff. This will quickly highlight the most frequent barriers to adoption and reveal opportunities to improve on today's situation.

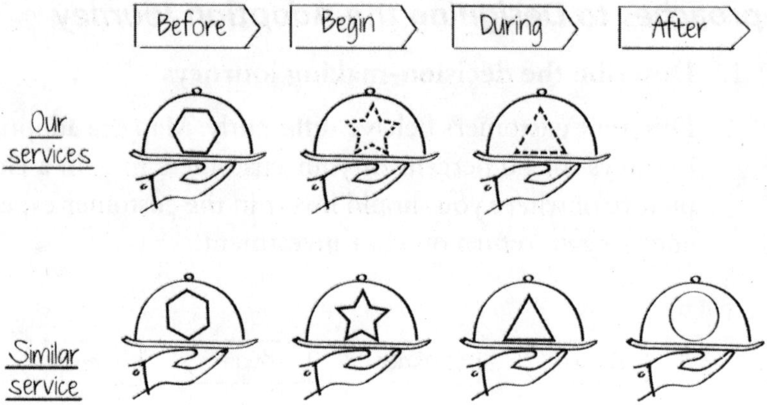

Similar services: *Compare and contrast your service experience with similar shortcuts to adoption solutions.*

3. **Design to remove unnecessary friction from customer's experience**

   Design new customer journeys and detail service specifications. Remove all unnecessary steps in the process, explain things that might be unclear to customers, and eliminate all potential irritations. Finally, design good confirmation routines to ensure that customers find that everything works smoothly, and feel they have made a good choice.

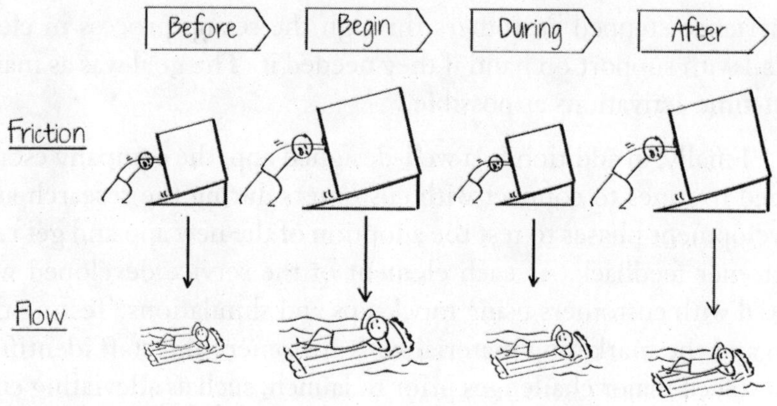

Friction and flow: *Understanding the points where customers may feel friction and how to support them to flow through the process will support greater adoption.*

How to Ensure a Successful Launch and Adoption in Practice

A leading telecom company decided to launch an innovative mobile payment service. Its focus was on designing an app that would make payment extremely clear and simple for customers.

Early on in the project, through customer testing, the team realized that the app would fail if they did not address critical customer issues occurring in the early stages of the customer journey (before phase). One issue was that new customers were uncertain about how they would keep an overview of their money when they paid using the new app instead of their card. This led the team to design marketing material that showed customers how they could manage their money using the phone.

Second, research of similar services showed that a significant percentage of customers would drop the service for good if they were not able to complete a transaction successfully on the first try. This led the team to design an industry-leading "out-of-the-box experience" to ensure that customers had a perfect start. This experience stepped customers through the set-up process in clear detail with support on hand if they needed it. The goal was as many first-time activations as possible.

Finally, in addition to a well-designed app, the company established routines to connect with customers during the research and development phases to test the adoption of the new app and get real customer feedback. As each element of the service developed was tested with customers using mock-ups and simulations. Testing the app and the marketing material with customers and staff identified and solved major challenges prior to launch, such as alleviating customer skepticism around the use of personal data. The Telco also set up routines to connect with customers a few weeks after launch to make sure customers were able to use the payment service—and help them get the most out of the payment service in their everyday life.

Takeaway Messages

1. Gain a deep understanding of the actors and factors that influence customers' experience and are beyond the control of the business to design a successful launch experience.
2. Map the key decision points in the consumer lifecycle to identify where you can drive adoption.
3. Invest in design elements that move customers through decision points in a good flow.
4. Design the experience *after* first use to drive sustainable adoption and gain return on investment.
5. Detail a customer adoption journey to understand barriers and hurdles.
6. Ensure the entire team has a shared view of what will enable customers to stick with the service over time.

Chapter 5

Organizational Challenge

Using Customer Centricity to Move Your Organization Forward

Services are delivered by organizations—public, private, big, and small. These organizations are made up of a number of different elements that come together to create value of some kind for customers and society. There are many ways to categorize the various elements of an organization: we often break it down into people, practices, processes, policies, and systems. We can also think of the classical breakdown into department or functions.

Large organizations exist in order to create value at scale, consistently and effectively. They often do this incredibly well. The organizational challenge is the challenge of doing things differently or changing things in an organization. The very qualities of scale, structure, and solidity that organizations have also make it hard to move things forward.

In many ways having a vision for a better customer experience or an innovative service is the easy bit. Getting it to happen in your organization is less easy. Service design is not simply about painting a picture of the bright future; it is also about rolling up your sleeves and making the change.

Service design offers a better understanding of customers and how to use this insight to engage people and structure strategies and plans. The approach looks at using customer stories to align activities between the departments of an organization. It describes how working with staff to improve their work and the work they do for customers can be more creative and rewarding. It also provides tools to expand on the idea of customer centricity and practical approaches to embedding it. Finally, we look at the challenge of speed and how to move an organization forward in a more agile fashion.

This section looks at four aspects of the organization challenge that we face in changing services. We explore how to develop an agile, customer-centric organization that is able to engage staff and align disparate functions in service of a common intention.

FOSTER INTERNAL ALIGNMENT AND COLLABORATION

One of the biggest challenges in introducing new propositions and services in the market is not the customer offer but the way the organization needs to prepare and organize internally. The organization, its teams, rewards, processes, and systems are usually structured in a way that creates and fosters silo thinking and behavior. Customer focus and insight brings an external perspective to an often very internal focused discussion and one factor—the customer—that all departments can align around. Using creative and design-oriented processes to analyze challenges and co-create solutions stimulates collaboration and creates alignment between departments.

When an organization attempts to introduce new or improved services it undergoes change. For a change to be successful the instigators of the change will need to take people with them. A new or improved service is likely to require collaboration between teams to deliver it and for each team to get clear on its part in that delivery. It is likely that each team will need to adapt its working practices and processes and essential that these practices align to create a coherent and well-functioning operation.

INSIGHTS

- Services are difficult to articulate clearly, and classic tools such as requirement specifications, business documents, and Project Initiation Documents (PIDs) do not communicate the desired experience. Visual representations of experiences in the form of scenarios that tell a story helps engage teams in a vision and solicit their involvement and contribution.
- Involving back office teams in customer experience work is hugely valuable—if rare. When we engage teams in service designs we find that they contribute a wealth of insight and ideas that improve the initial concepts and inspires the development of more effective back office practices.
- Collaboration and alignment can be achieved quickly with good facilitation and design tools. Bringing the right people into a room and structuring their input leads to rapid developments.

Why Read On?

- Learn how to align your organization around new or improved services.
- See how collaboration can be quick and high impact.
- Understand how to align around customer experience.

Internal Alignment and Collaboration

The success of the service will depend on the alignment of teams and how they contribute to making services as good as possible. The lack of collaboration and alignment between teams or functions—silos—is a common challenge when organizations attempt to change. This becomes an issue when customers' needs and expectations are not met due to different departments pulling in different directions, and with different priorities. A classic example is when a critical department—say IT or legal—has not been involved in the service design, and their translation of requirements fails to deliver the optimal experience to customers by placing an additional burden on the customer or barriers to their achieving their goals. Think about when you have had to try to understand paperwork, complete an onerous form, or wait for a painful process. IT systems can literally prevent staff from doing the right thing for customers by codifying poor experiences. When your frontline staff does not understand a new service, they will not talk about it with knowledge or conviction.

Businesses that bring cross-functional teams together to focus on how they each support the creation of customer value build a different kind of organizational strength. This approach develops an explicit understanding of shared purpose. Each department or function understands the role it plays in ensuring that value is created effectively. Building on a shared purpose, cross-functional teams can understand where the specific challenge lies in creating customer value. This enables them to focus on improving or rethinking specific areas in line with the overall vision. Better interactions between functions result in better alignment and collaboration, which results in delivering customer value as well as business effectiveness.

How to Collaboratively Develop Scenarios to Align Teams or Functions

Customers' experience, and specifically the design of how customers should be able to move through the customer lifecycle, is a hugely powerful tool to align roles, departments, or functions. In many ways customers, and the value your organization is creating for them, is the only common ground that can be shared by every function across the business. If you and your team are not contributing to value creation for customers, then you may be creating waste work, or worse, reducing value by preventing customers from achieving their needs or goals.

To tackle a challenging service design project, you need to put together a cross-functional team covering strategic, operational, management, and frontline colleagues. It is important to establish clear sponsorship of this way of working as traditional hierarchies need to be relaxed and people need to be comfortable with a more collaborative working style. The first step for your new cross-functional team is to establish a shared understanding of customer needs and expectations. This can be achieved by collaboratively undertaking customer research—literally getting the back office out in the customers' world. It is valuable to document real customer experiences as video and testimonials backed up by hard behavioral data. This provides the understanding that fuels alignment around customer needs.

Once you are clear on your insights into customer needs and expectations you can begin to develop a target scenario for how the service could perform better. The target scenarios you develop should be well aware of the business goals for your service and the specific performances or outcomes you are aiming to achieve. By mapping the key organizational functions effected by the scenario, you can systematically work through each area and discuss the impact the scenario has on that role.

When you have a target scenario for the customer experience you can begin to unpack the impact that this scenario will have on different areas of the organization. By literally plotting parallel activities across functions and teams—say, marketing, sales, operations and legal,—you will see who is doing what when and be able to discuss together how this is contributing to or impairing the target customer experience. It is essential while doing this to capture the discussion. Service blueprints are a great tool for this because they are very structured and assist in aligning the roles of different teams to the customer experience. Blueprints can be drawn on whiteboards or plotted on the wall to create a shared view and focus. Later they must be captured as a key requirement document.

Undertaking this exercise will bring up a range of issues and opportunities. It is important to capture and structure these—they will inform project plans and road maps for taking action. It is unlikely that you establish either the perfect target customer experience or a clear picture of the organizational change requirements on first pass. Expect to continue a dialogue that moves between tweaking the target experience and challenging the organizational barriers. Once a team has been brought together and shared in the scenario development it will be much easier to work in smaller teams on specific tasks. It is, however, advisable to bring the big group back to key points.

Approaches to Help Create Scenarios for Alignment and Collaboration

1. **Aligning around the customer story**

   Service design uses visualization to create a shared understanding of customer experience and value. To use this scenario to align teams around and enable delivery of the target customer experience it is important to define what the critical success factors are for the customer at each stage. These factors can then be discussed with teams to understand their roles in enabling success.

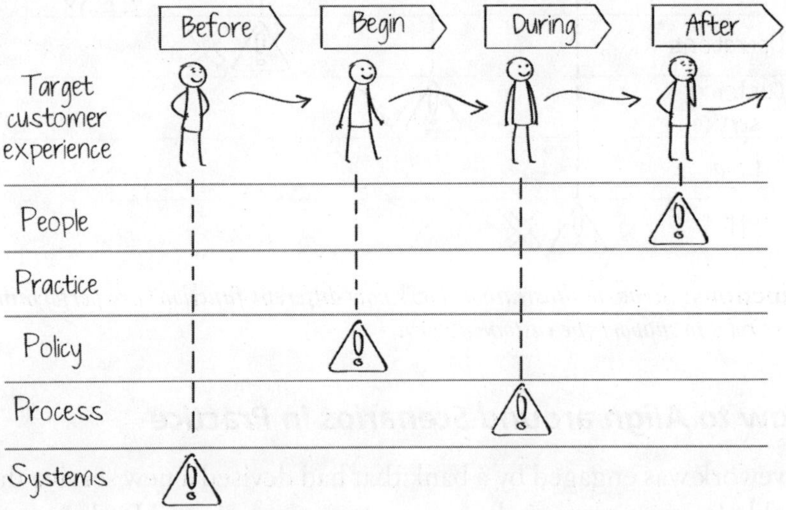

Success factors: *Scenario illustration shows a target customer experience and defined critical success factors in achieving the vision.*

2. **Aligning around the business story**

   Once you have an idea of what a target customer experience should be and the critical success factors, you can analyze the requirements placed on each functional area of the business. This can enable you to be clear about who does what when. You may find that some areas are too hard to resolve quickly. If so, this can be fed back into the customer engagement design to ensure that the target experience is realistic and achievable.

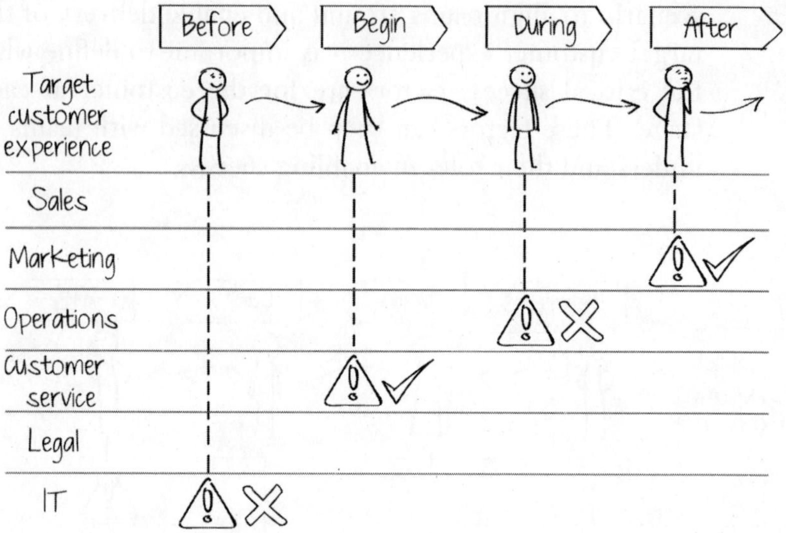

Functions: *Scenario illustration shows how different functions are performing their roles to support the customer story.*

How to Align around Scenarios in Practice

Livework was engaged by a bank that had devised a new service that enabled customers to make payments more easily and for less transactional cost. Research showed that this service was hugely desirable. However, the service required consumers to create a viable market for merchants to adopt the system. The bank needed to drive adoption quickly.

The bank had tried a traditional way to address this challenge, advertising. The marketing team had taken a traditional approach and spent a lot of money plastering posters for the service across the city. This had failed to make a dent in adoption. The bank needed to take a different approach and examined the customer experience of their new payment service.

Through interviews with customers at the branch and in shopping streets, it quickly became clear that a customer seeing the advertisement was highly unlikely to adopt the service due to multiple barriers, including the need to physically sign up at a branch, complete a complex form, and wait for authorization. With this insight it was easy to design a better, smoother experience for customers.

The challenge the bank then faced was to deliver on this improved design. The new approach required changes from the legal team for the terms and conditions, IT for the processing, operations for the branch activity, and more. By getting these departments into the room, sharing the "as is" and "to be" customer experience designs and asking "How can you contribute to making this happen?," the bank was able to define an action plan across departments to make this new service stand a chance in the future. This was done in two days because of two factors: the obvious collaboration in one room and the visualization of how each department needed to support the customer through the adoption stage of the new service. The teams developed ideas for better ways to do their work, or to challenge established practices, for the benefit of the customer experience. They also identified ways to save work costs or to improve their processes and systems. Within two days the bank had a new strategy and an action plan to implement it.

Takeaway Messages

1. Customer experience scenarios enable alignment around a clear vision.
2. Engaging teams across the organization leads to additional process and practice innovation.
3. Alignment can be quick and effective using service design tools.
4. Once teams are aligned they can work independently on specific tasks.

DELIVER BETTER STAFF ENGAGEMENT AND PARTICIPATION

Digital channels, customer experience prioritization, and cost drivers require that people in service businesses change the work that they do. These major trends are having a huge impact on the roles and activities of frontline staff in almost every service sector. For most people change is unwelcome. Change comes with uncertainty, fear, and skepticism. It is essential to manage these challenges in any change and counter doubt and worry with clarity and purpose.

The creative, visual storytelling and collaborative aspects of service design offer a different more participatory way to engage staff in changes. In addition, this approach can bring out the best of staff, drawing on their knowledge, experience, and practical common sense.

INSIGHTS

- Engagement delivered by consultants is not ideal for most people. They want to have the discussions within their organization, with peers and managers, unmediated. Designing a program that trains a core team to take a program delivery role works best.

- It is likely that some strategic goals will feel too sensitive to share as they may trigger adverse reactions. However, anything withheld is likely to become the "elephant in the room" and inhibit the process. Better out than in as a rule.

Why Read On?

- Understand how to creatively engage staff in change.
- Learn how to manage a staff engagement using a design process.
- See how a service design approach can scale.

Staff Engagement and Participation

By staff we are referring to people who interact with customers as part of their job. From salespeople to customer service reps, field engineers, advisors, and even consultants, staff roles vary enormously but they all have customer interaction in common.

For large organizations staff can be a large number of people. A particular role can be held by tens of thousands of people across a global organization. This means that engaging staff can be a large and daunting task. However, if a change is desired and it requires people to change their roles, then there must be some engagement. The best engagement does not just inform and require change but solicits insight, ideas, and feedback from staff to ensure that the change is optimized. Staff should be engaged early in change by asking *them*: What needs to change? And what should we do to improve? This approach enables better understanding of issues and opportunities, better options and solutions, and on top of this, it counters the uncertainty and skepticism. Staff will feel included and aware of the issues, options, and decisions made along the way.

In addition to engagement, staff can be hugely valuable participants in change, improvement, or innovation work. Usually decisions are undertaken at a strategic level and then handed down to delivery functions to implement, where they hit issues and often need rework or can fail. Government suffers from this acutely as there is often a huge gap between policy makers and delivery organizations—they are often different organizations altogether. Staff knowledge, developed through experience on the front line, is a goldmine of insight and ideas for how to improve. It can also be the best and quickest test bed for plans and ideas before investments are made.

There may be real tensions between the business and staff around changes that involve their roles or even cuts in jobs. The natural, and sometimes legally essential, approach in these cases is one of secrecy. However, in highly charged cases, where industrial relations are fraught, engagement is even more important and an open, collaborative, and creative approach even more valuable. There is no shortcut to doing this; it requires bravery and the belief that it is a better way forward.

How to Work with Staff Collaboratively and Creatively But with Structure and at Scale

The way to engage staff creatively, within a structure that sets boundaries, is to take them through a customer-centered design process. Design uses clear phases that enable teams to come together and develop insights, ideas, tests, and solutions. We call these phases *Understand*, *Imagine*, *Design*, and *Create*. In this case, the role of staff members is being designed in response to this change.

By starting with *understanding* you are engaging staff members in the process of understanding their role in relation to the customers that they are there to serve, and the business that they work for. Using customer journey tools to discuss customer experience with staff solicits their insight into this experience and where it could improve. They will also contribute the pain points they have in trying to meet customer needs, uncovering additional insights and opportunities.

The second thing for staff to understand is the business agenda or strategy. If there are pressures on the business then they should be introduced, be they cost, performance, or competition. If there are technology trends, these should be shared. If there is a need to rise to the challenge of competition, this should be exposed. The business should share their options for future service delivery. If done with transparency most staff will see the logic and be less resistant.

Once an understanding is established then the process can move into imagining how roles and activities can change. Staff teams can develop new scenarios where they describe their changing role in response to both customers and the business. These scenarios should describe the new service with a focus on roles. This phase produces a range of options that can be fed into the business change process.

At this point, staff teams need to work with business teams to refine these scenarios into a more developed design that can be taken forward. These designs can be detailed and tested in prototype environments such as role-playing spaces or dummy service environments. This phase is very valuable as staff teams get a feel of the future job and their role.

It is important to acknowledge that in a change process there will be teams across the business designing different aspects of the future-operating model. These teams may be focused on technologies, organization, or environments, for example. To do their jobs effectively these teams should interface with staff processes and teams at key points to input their thinking and to get feedback. They will need to negotiate between options and be transparent about decisions. This can be a challenge and can feel like adding time and effort, but it will pay off. Ideally some of the staff team members should join these work streams and contribute directly.

It is important that engagement or participation is a structured process with clear timelines, lines of communication, and progress toward a solution. This structure balances the elements of openness and creativity. It also provides clarity about the form of engagement and participation. Not all staff members can contribute to all phases and work streams, but if they are clear about how their voice is being represented by others and there is good communication down the line, they will trust the process.

When a staff body is large or distributed, it is not possible to have total participation for all. An engagement design need not aim for this but for reasonable involvement at different levels. A good starting point is for a core staff team, which is representative of different perspectives, to be highly involved. This team will become the face of the project. This team can reach significant numbers delivering high-touch engagement with teams across locations, work streams, or roles. These engagement sessions are service design activities as described earlier and should be co-designed with the core team. If a core team can reach tens or hundreds then this second layer of engagement can reach the majority of its colleagues through activities and communications between attendees and their day-to-day colleagues using the outputs of collaborative sessions to share the work with others.

Approaches for Using Design Processes for Engagement

1. **Structuring a creative engagement program**

   The design process provides the structure to enable engagement of staff in change through clear phases and in response to customer and business factors. It systematically moves them from understanding to designing new working practices and enables testing and acceptance before implementation.

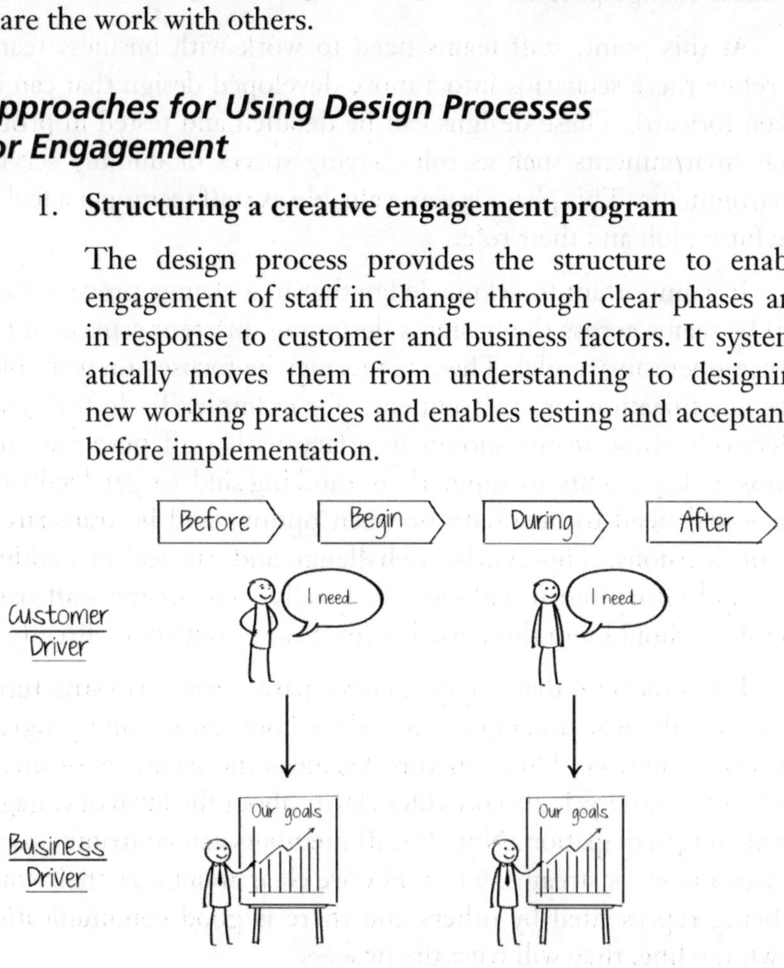

Customer and business: *How staff teams can be taken through a design process to engage them in change by considering both customer and business drivers.*

2. **Designing roles in response to customers and business**
   In this approach, staffs become service designers with a focus on their roles. They should be encouraged to do this in dialogue with customer needs and business needs and understand that this is a negotiation. This will enable them to create scenarios where they can tell the story of the new roles and develop test activities where these roles can be experienced.

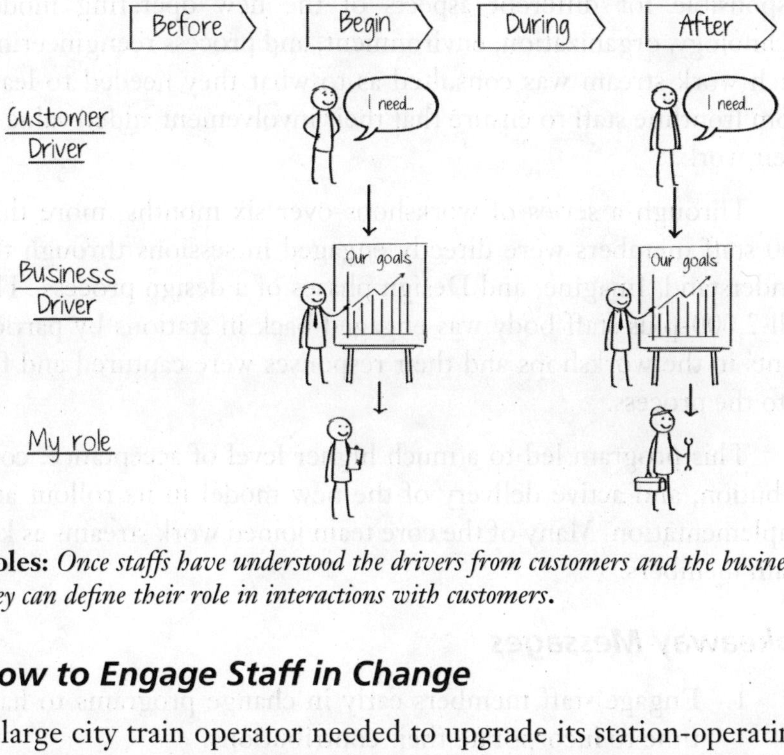

Roles: *Once staffs have understood the drivers from customers and the business, they can define their role in interactions with customers.*

How to Engage Staff in Change

A large city train operator needed to upgrade its station-operating model in response to three key business drivers—new ticketing technology reducing demand for a ticket office, growing pressure on customer experience excellence, and a need to reduce operating costs based on high staff numbers. This operator has a highly unionized workforce, a history of strikes, and a need to be very careful about changes to roles and jobs.

The Managing Director of the operator understood that staff engagement was key and that a new approach was needed. In fact, he had publicly promised to do it differently. There was a need and appetite for a more participatory approach. Livework had been involved in the station vision and was asked to design the engagement of staff.

A team of station staff and supervisors were recruited to form a core service design team and to run the engagement program. This team designed activities with staff for face-to-face workshops and peer-to-peer communications to those not directly engaged.

The team also worked alongside the change work streams responsible for different aspects of the new operating model: technology, organization, environment, and process reengineering. Each work stream was consulted as to what they needed to learn from frontline staff to ensure that their involvement added value to their work.

Through a series of workshops over six months, more than 800 staff members were directly engaged in sessions through the Understand, Imagine, and Design phases of a design process. The full 2,000-plus staff body was engaged back in stations by participants in the workshops and their responses were captured and fed into the process.

This program led to a much higher level of acceptance, contribution, and active delivery of the new model in its rollout and implementation. Many of the core team joined work streams as key team members.

Takeaway Messages

1. Engage staff members early in change programs to have time to incorporate their contributions.
2. Staff insight into day-to-day practice is invaluable to service redesign and implementation of new operating models.
3. Use a design approach to engage staff and enable staff to understand and contribute better to the new model.
4. Participative engagement works in a range of environments, from highly collaborative teams to stressed industrial environments.

BUILD A CUSTOMER-CENTRIC ORGANIZATION

Someone once said, "Our organization is so complex that the only one who can see the bigger picture is our customer." This seems to apply to many people working in corporate silos striving to put the customer at the top of the agenda.

Uniting the organization around a common view of what matters for customers can result in huge rewards for businesses. Companies such as Virgin, Amazon, and Zappos have demonstrated the rewards of being truly customer-centric organizations, breeding loyalty and doing more business with customers. One factor that distinguishes these businesses is that they were set up as customer-centric organizations from day one. Unfortunately, most businesses do not have the privilege of starting from scratch. Most will need to change well-established (industrial) organizations away from a focus on products and processes to a focus on customers, keeping the customer at the heart of everything they do.

A service design approach has proven to be a powerful tool to define a customer-centric vision and turn it into a concrete reality for staff and customers. The approach helps to simplify complex situations, sometimes through visualization, other times by bringing attention to the surprisingly obvious truths. It offers tools to create customer strategies by connecting insight to actions—and supports in identifying the actions that will create the most impact.

> **INSIGHTS**
>
> - Senior management that truly believes in the value of customer centricity is essential to success. If they're not on board, lower your ambitions on behalf of customers.
> - Build customer-orientation programs that enable change within "the business as usual." Keep consultants at the fringes of activities, fund activities from the usual budgets, and engage people in it as continual improvement, not special projects.
> - Do not waste time building a detailed business case for customer centricity. A good high-level case for business success combined with a good human story is the strongest bet to convince stakeholders.

Why Read On?

- Learn how to develop a customer-centric organization using service design as an approach.
- Understand how to go from a vision to reality for customers and staff.
- See how service design can be most powerful to engage the organization.

Put Customers at the Center of the Business

In simple terms, customer centricity means that the organization has made it a clear business choice to prioritize great experiences for customers, and gives employees the resources to deliver it. Developing a customer-centric organization requires a strategic decision to engage people at all levels of the organization to put customers first, and a strong rationale to back it. Shifting the focus to customers, and away from products, can have quick and broad impact but requires serious commitment to training and a willingness to take on changes needed in the way the organization works.

Customer centricity can be led from the top down or grown from the bottom up. Often, the most dramatic changes come from the top when leadership truly empathizes with customers. The idea of the CEO as "Chief Customer Officer" is a strong one, and a design approach can be highly effective in helping leaders to gain increased empathy with customers' experience of the business.

In one example, a management team needed to connect to the reality customers experienced with their cable TV company. To make this happen, design team members presented a set of artificial personas with pictures, quotes, and insights that represented the customer segmentation of the company. They engaged the managers in a discussion about what could be done to increase customer satisfaction. The conversation reflected market research insight as well as commonly held opinions about potential actions, mostly focused on product improvement (channel packages) and price. The surprise was great during the next session, when it turned out that the personas were not only real individuals, but the design team had brought them to the session to be interviewed, and listened to, by the managers. The surprise grew even more when managers realized how little the channel packages impacted on the customer experience. It turned out that customers felt great irritation connected to poorly designed setup processes, which made it difficult for people to even use the content as intended and reduced loyalty to the company. Even more worryingly, customers were considering dropping cable TV altogether in favor of streaming content using the Internet.

In the end, everyone on the management team had a personal experience of what *really* made a difference to *real* people who paid for their services, and gained the clarity, urgency, and focus required to make a shift to more customer-oriented ways to perform better.

When businesses take on the challenge of making the customer experience prime priority, they need to engage "the head, hands, and heart" of people in the organization. There needs to be clear logic as to why the customer matters to the business and people must be equipped with the necessary tools, skills, and knowledge—and most importantly they must be emotionally engaged in the mission. The process of change to elevate customer awareness across an organization involves a number of different change-management competencies. A service design approach complements these competencies and provides highly effective approaches to engage stakeholders across the organization, reveal customer insights, and turn these into impactful actions.

How to Build a Customer-Centric Organization

Once a company decides to move from a customer-oriented vision and strategy to implementation, action (change) is required across the organization. Service design can help businesses develop customer strategies. It provides tools to structure and combine insights, create an action plan by addressing improvements across the customer lifecycle, and describe the desired experience using a visual map. The approach also enables engagement and involvement across departments and teams.

Service design offers language and tools to understand and discuss the customer experience in more human and precise ways, making it a helpful approach to engage stakeholders across the organization. Terms like the customer journey enable people to think about the customer experience step-by-step—and service blueprints, for example, allow teams to get an overview of how an experience is delivered.

Basic service design training enables executives, leaders, teams, and specialists to gain shared references, logic, and stories that can be shared with a wider audience. Ambassadors that are "customer-experience literate" are crucial to success in engaging the organization at large.

Once a certain level of knowledge is established, the stage is set to carry through acts that heighten awareness with broader teams and create a small but powerful set of quick wins and examples everyone will talk about.

A systematic approach to customer centricity requires a robust setup before it can be implemented. To get ready, there are a few basic foundations that will help to build a strong platform and form a strategy for what the business wants to do with customers.

The first element is to gain a solid foundation of customer insight. Much of this will be found in existing business data such as market surveys, customer satisfaction surveys, and in sales, operations, and defection data. Usually data lives in different parts of the business and needs to be collated to give a unified picture of customers' needs, wants, irritations, and problems.

In addition, it will pay off to conduct qualitative customer research to complement quantitative data. Sometimes this can bring up whole new perspectives that are invisible when you just look at behavior through data. Another benefit is that the results provide tangible human stories that bring data to life as real experiences. Finally, there is huge potential in taking staff at various levels out of the office to observe and interview customers in their context. Even though doing firsthand research can be hard to prioritize in a busy schedule, it rarely fails to bring personal excitement and an urgency to get better and helps team members to interpret other data better.

The second element is to describe customer lifecycles and create an outside-in view of their behavior with the industry and the company. Phase-by-phase maps of what customers experience make it possible to distinguish where you can make the greatest difference, seen from a customer perspective. Most important of all, it is a way to establish and communicate a common view of the business as seen through the eyes of customers.

Third, creating a set of customer personas helps to build a platform for action. These abstracts represent typical customers and describe them as people in a story format including needs and desired outcomes. Personas are a helpful guide when you wish to engage teams in solving problems with the customer at the center. They can anchor and guide conversations and bring clarity to important questions such as "Would John really pay more for this?," or "Can Wendy really make use of this?"

Business Plan

Customer insight, customer lifecycles, and tangible customer personas make it possible to form a strategy focused on customers. It enables you to identify, communicate, and prioritize what, when, and how the business can increase value for customers. The next step is to set ambitious goals for success with customers and build an actionable plan to achieve them.

Often organizations struggle to balance customer needs with business needs. Even though the customer need is clear, it can be hard to judge the return on investment of satisfying it. Even trickier, how will one improvement to the customer experience pay off more than another?

The customer lifecycle offers a way to see beyond fixing a particular customer issue and focuses on root causes and effects. For example, customer defection, triggered by irritation and confusion over a bill, is not necessarily avoided by designing a clearer bill. The answer can be to redesign service packages in a prepurchase phase making them simpler to understand for customers. This is likely to increase sales as well as reduce call center traffic from confused customers and ultimately boost loyalty through a hassle-free experience.

The service design approach helps to identify *hotspots* at particular stages in the customer lifecycle. These hotspots mark specific behaviors where customers will find value in a better experience, and where the business can reduce costs or increase revenues. The lifecycle view offers a clear picture of where root causes (of the hotspots) occur, often in other stages of the lifecycle. This view also makes it possible to identify high-impact interventions to eliminate problems or drive behaviors that make a positive mark on the bottom line.

Building on clear hotspots, it is possible to analyze organizational challenges involved in realizing interventions. Implications across different departments, systems, and processes can be financial, political, legal, or technical. By flagging these challenges, it is possible to understand the real cost of improvement.

Using the customer lifecycle as a tool to identify action and judge return on investment compared to value for customers puts the business in a better place to build a customer-oriented business strategy.

With a clear strategy for customers and a clear strategy for the business, it is possible to set in motion actions across the organization that will pay off for both. This foundation provides a solid basis for engaging staff across an organization with a clear and shared picture of challenges to solve.

Implementation

Service design really proves its value when it is time to implement customer centricity because it helps to bridge strategy and customer knowledge with the design of the service experience.

A typical example is the design of systems and processes that enable staff to deliver better with customers. In one example a company implemented a highly advanced CRM system and integrated it into call center software for staff. It turned out that access to extremely detailed customer data did not enable a better experience with customers. A design team came in armed with customer insight and redesigned the staff computer interface to facilitate the best possible dialogue built on the data. The effort to implement it was low, but the effects were immediate and brought satisfaction both to customers and staff.

It also pays off to apply service design as a way to involve staff and customers in developing concrete solutions. On the road to customer centricity, co-design can make a great difference because it engages staff to think and act in hands-on ways to improve the customer experience. Prototyping and piloting new service experiences with staff helps realize the best interventions and at the same time makes them enthusiastic and active proponents for change.

Approaches for Developing a Customer-Centric Organization

1. **Mapping hotspots to the lifecycle**

   Hotspots can be defined as the sum of customer pain and business impact. If the customer pain is high and it is causing a significant business issue, then the hotspot is severe and worth addressing.

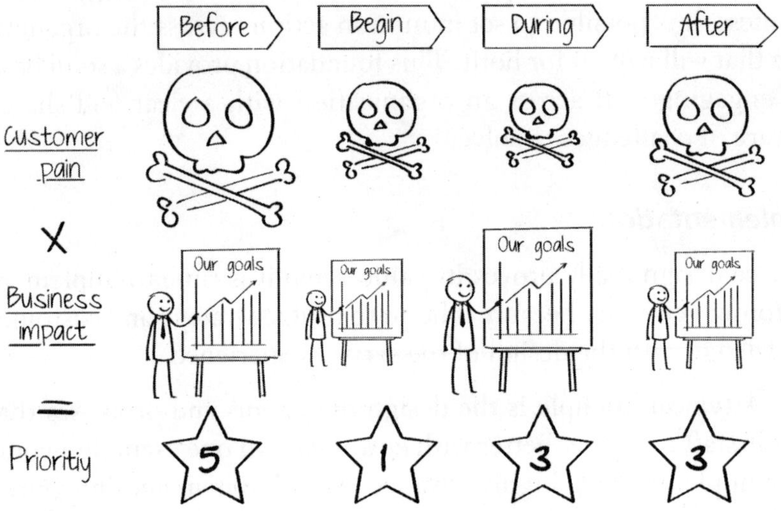

Hotspots: *By scoring the level of customer pain and business impact, an overall ranking of hotspots can be established.*

How to Create a Customer-Centric Organization in Practice

The leadership of a dominant financial company made a decision to prioritize customer centricity and move it to the top of the agenda in response to recognizing that "customers are the entire reason we are here."

They created a customer-orientation program and organized a kick-off event where the CEO of the company assembled his top 100 managers to set the agenda. During the event everyone was given a list of 10 random customers and asked to call them and truly listen to what they thought about the company. Many of the managers were positively surprised at how well the company was appreciated by customers. The conversation also revealed some obvious problems for customers that undoubtedly needed to be fixed to meet expectations. In any case, everyone in the room had a personal experience of what customers did and did not appreciate. The direction to put the customer first was tangible, personal, and clear.

They also established a set of principles to ensure financial success and sustainability beyond the program period:

- The program was led by two highly trusted officers in the company.
- This small team engaged selected customer ambassadors in each department of the organization.
- Every department in the business was required to deliver several customer improvements.
- All actions were funded in the line, not by extraordinary program budgets.
- External consultants were not involved, except for in a few particular areas of expertise, such as service design.
- A measurement system was set up to measure customer satisfaction in all customer-facing channels.
- Customer satisfaction metrics were shared with teams and individual staff, and continual training was established to help improve performance on an individual basis.

The next step toward becoming a truly customer-oriented company was removing any detail that could irritate customers. The organization implemented 183 improvements to the service experience over two years. Some were small fixes; others required significant rethinking of how services were delivered. This broad range of activities involved nearly every employee in the process and set the organization on a continual quest to create a better customer experience.

Delivering a great customer experience requires a keen sense of the company's true identity. To boost this, the company launched an internal branding program as a framework for customer orientation. A comprehensive training program established clear principles for all employees on how they should make a difference to customers.

Combined with nearly 200 service improvements, this created a trustworthy platform for external brand renewal. When the company gained confidence that it could deliver on a truly customer-oriented promise, it took the leap from a traditional corporate expression to an immediately identifiable, expressive, and colorful platform for telling human stories. The company is now a true "service brand"— the brand is embedded in the service experience.

Four years after the completion of the program, the company has the facts that prove the value of its commitment. In ratings, the company has moved from ranking in the 70s to the top 10 of customer satisfaction nationally independently of industry, a rare feat for a financial company. Numerous awards for customer experience excellence give the company recognition for its efforts.

More significantly, systematic measurements also prove the effects on the bottom line. The numbers prove that customers are more satisfied than before, and more satisfied than with competitors. The company brings in new customers and they stay loyal longer. The most significant financial impact is that the most satisfied customers spend a lot more with a provider they trust. This pays off when close to 90 percent of customers are satisfied.

Takeaway Messages

1. The sum of many small customer-oriented actions can produce massive business results.
2. Customer orientation drives results on the bottom line in terms of sales, customer value, and loyalty.
3. Highly satisfied customers grow their spending massively with favored service providers.

BUILDING A MORE AGILE ORGANIZATION

Quick change requires agility. To be able to create quickly, to be able to try, fail, learn, and adapt requires agility. But many organizations are designed to be the opposite, firm and steady, and focused on consistent and efficient delivery. How do we bring the former to the latter?

Service design implies improvement or innovation, which requires change and creativity. By creativity we mean the ability to make something new. This is an approach that suits large organizations as it brings a mix of structure and fluidity to bear on their challenges. It enables creativity and divergent thinking but also synthesis, prioritization, and consideration of the implications of change.

> **INSIGHTS**
>
> - The assumption is often that the hard changes are also the high-impact ones. Focusing on the easier solutions first can have the surprising effect of making some of the harder issues disappear.
> - Agility can often be thought of as primarily to do with culture and being the property of younger companies. More important is senior sponsorship and clarity of purpose to prevent blockers from slowing the process. Get the CEO on board.

Why Read On?

- Understand how to use a lifecycle to structure a development road map.
- Learn how to categorize changes into levels to aid multi-speed development.

Agility in Response to Customer Demand and Technology

Many large organizations lack clear leadership of what they do with customers—it may exist, fragmented across different areas, but that is not leadership. Assuming that serving customers is ultimately the purpose of the organization, this is a very odd situation.

Most organizations are structured in functional departments or silos: sales, marketing, operations, and so on. In addition to this, other functions provide capabilities to these teams: technology, finance, HR, and so on. These structures reinforce the stability but hamper agility as initiatives must cross the silos.

An agile organization is one that is able to move forward with some fluidity and adaptability. It is able to respond to changes in the market, customer expectations, or technology in a smart and efficient manner. We are not talking about culture as much as having an established practice that enables decisions to be made, new things tried, failures learned from, and success grown.

There are two related areas that service design specifically helps to develop more agile organizations, in response to customer demands and in using technology to meet these demands.

In mature economies, the nature of customer demand has changed. People are more independent and individualistic than they used to be, and their expectations have developed in line to expect greater personal service and personalization. Customers are better informed as they have greater than ever access to information from the web on the value, quality, and performance of products and services. Customers switch providers or make their voices heard when they do not get what they expect. Large businesses and government services lag behind. Many still employ the large bureaucratic structures and processes of a previous era where more power was held by the organization, which was trusted more and questioned less. Customers have become more agile in their ability to navigate and choose, and it is time that service providers catch up.

Technological progress has gone hand in hand with this customer development. In many ways technology enables more informed customers to access information quickly and when they need it. It has also spawned a number of new business models that have shown customers what is possible. Technology also enables services to be more personal as customer data can be held and used to deliver a personalized experience while still delivering services to thousands of people. New digital technology challenges older technologies that were designed to manage and control consistency and scale, rather than enable personalization and adaptability.

The challenge is to become agile when starting in a risk-averse and control-driven context. A service design approach will enable you to assess and mitigate risks and provide control of a creative process, all to enable development of services that customers want.

How to Develop a More Agile Approach to Service Delivery

To become a more agile organization—better able to respond to changing customer needs and exploit new technologies—you need to develop a clear, shared view of what you deliver to customers and how each area of the business plays a role in delivery. You also need to understand how well you deliver on all things you do with customers and ensure that you help your customers achieve their goals. A service design approach can help to develop this picture of what you do with customers. It then provides tools to reveal the least well-performing area and improve that performance.

To do this we start with a customer lifecycle—the lifecycle provides a framework that structures and categorizes the things you do with customers. We use the lifecycle as a scenario-building or storytelling tool to force an outside-in perspective and map what the organization does to deliver what customers need and experience. For example, what do you do to attract customers? What do you do to support them when they join? Establish measures of performance at each stage of the lifecycle as well as overall performance goals to help to identify the priority areas for customers. Using a lifecycle in this way provides the first step to a more agile and responsive approach to service improvement and management.

The next step is to map the areas of high or low performance against clear customer needs using existing or new customer insight data. Customer needs can be broken down into three areas: needs for *information*, *interaction*, and *transactions*. Better understanding customer needs (for information, interaction, and transaction) helps to identify when and how to respond to customers to meet their needs. This is hugely valuable as it enables you to move at different speeds for different needs. Responding to a need for information (say, when a customer needs a better explanation of a product) is an easier task than responding to a need for a simpler transaction (such as a reworked contract). By splitting these three needs categories apart you will be able to take action on each level knowing that there will be different speeds of development and resolution. What we are aiming for is a three-speed approach to change that decouples these three levels of customer need, enabling you to move fast to progress the easier informational improvements while recognizing that the transactional changes you desire may take longer.

Customers need information to make decisions and to stay in control of their service contract and usage. They also need the information that you provide to be clear and usable in order to be reassured that things are right or to do their part in ensuring that a service achieves its outcomes. Customers who do not understand services due to poor information do not buy, make greater numbers of calls for help, are less satisfied overall, and get in the way. The general truth is that organizations present information from the inside-out to customers using organization language that the customer does not understand. Energy customers struggle with kilowatt hours for example. It is not hard to uncover the language that customer use. Spending time with them and recording the way they talk about services and their needs will give you the customer voice. A simple example is that customers talk about energy in terms of the money it costs, not the scientific measure.

Once information needs are identified, they can generally be resolved quickly. Solutions can be changes to language, presentation, or simple access that enables customers to get the information they need and understand it better. This is a relatively simple task that organizations can do without changing core systems, processes, or policy. Information can also be disseminated extremely easily with today's technology landscape. Social media and aggregation services offer mechanisms to distribute information. Knowing customer informational needs enables you to start the first track of the three-speed approach, providing customers with better information. This will provide early benefits in a range of forms. For example, you may achieve fewer customer requests for information, freeing up human resources for higher value work.

The next level of customer need is for *interactions*. Interactions are exchanges between customers and agents of the organization or business. A consultation is a classic interaction for many services from health care to financial services. These interactions enable customers to apply the services capabilities to themselves through a two-way interaction. Interactions help customers make decisions and feel reassured that they also often provide the core tangible aspect of the service that provides value to the customer. Interactions were classically face-to-face but more and more have moved onto telephone and digital channels. We see that the high-touch interactions remain human, but more routine interactions can be codified into digital tools like wizards, forms, and apps. We can define the interactions that customers require by understanding where they need additional expertise. There are areas in services where there is specialist knowledge that customers generally will not have. These are the areas where interactions are needed to guide customers through. Different types of customers will have different levels of needs in this area (we often map how savvy different customer groups are to help differentiate needs). These points of interaction needs can be mapped to the lifecycle. Bear in mind that some interaction needs can be met by educating customers to be self-sufficient next time.

Interactions are harder to change, but they are not hardwired into the systems or policies of an organization. Generally, processes or practices govern interactions, and a business trains people to perform them. Take two examples: a maintenance visit from an engineer or a call to a call center to rent a car. Both of these interactions are planned for, and the agent uses a planned practice or script. They are repeatable and represent the moment where the customer provides critical inputs such as what is wrong with the boiler or when they would like the car.

These interactions can differ hugely in quality without changing the core. The engineer could be purely functional in his approach, do the job, and get out, or he could be more sympathetic with the customers and clear about what he has done and how they can maintain their system. The second will lead to much happier customers who may even maintain their boiler better and reduce future call outs. Design ways to support agents to undertake these interactions in the best way possible by providing tools that enable them to do the job well.

Transactions, and the fear of changing them, are often what hold organizations back from moving in a more agile manner. Setting up a customer on a system and dealing with their payments and defaults has to be robust and stable. Once these systems are established and the interdependencies of different functions wired in then a change could have a significant knock-on effect and require time and money to adapt. The ultimate expression of this situation is in the frustration with a legacy system that restricts a business from doing what it wants but is too big to change. The danger with these systems is that their structures, and in some cases messes, are reflected externally onto the customer experience.

Transactional improvements sometimes feel like monumental tasks—and the impact the change has means they are all saved up for a system upgrade in the future. To avoid this fate it can be beneficial to break the transactions down into small steps and improve elements of them at a time, picking the elements that have high feasibility. Each micro improvement can have a positive impact with the additional benefit of not disrupting the whole operation and the risks of system changes.

Approaches to Agile Organizations

1. **Structuring for agile decisions**

   Using the categories of information, interaction, and transaction can help clarify what kind of need customers have to develop strategies to move forward on three fronts at different speeds.

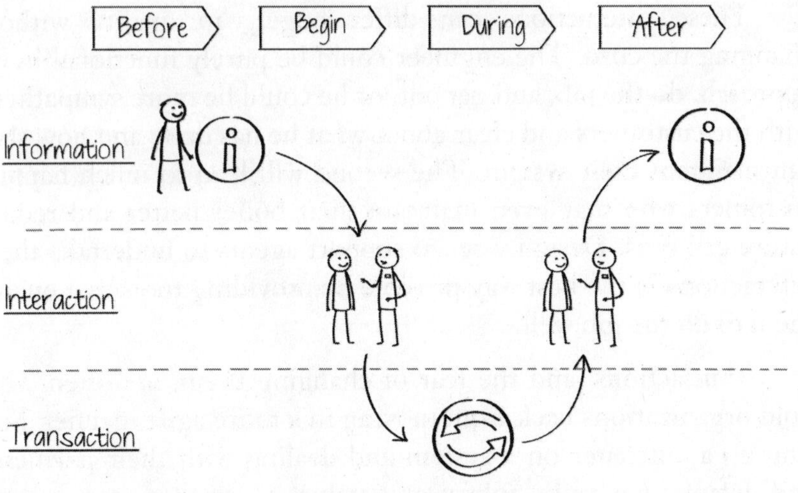

Information, interaction, transaction: *How staff teams can be taken through a design process to engage them in change.*

How to Be More Agile in a Challenging Context

A large manufacturing company of equipment used in large buildings (monitoring systems and end-point sensors) realized that growth in their sector was in services. Due to a mature market and declining product margins, services that maintain and upgrade systems for customers are growing and more profitable.

Customers had become more demanding and their expectations had been raised by experiences they were having elsewhere with other service companies. The firm needed to adapt quickly to retain its existing customer base, reduce rising churn, and maintain its premium status in the market that had been established through product quality.

Working with Livework, the firm engaged with customers to understand their core needs from the services and to develop a strategy to improve and grow the services business. This work developed a new set of propositions based on customer needs and opportunities.

While the propositions were widely accepted and bought into, the organization faced a range of barriers due to the current situation of the business. Adopting the strategy felt like a wholesale change at an organizational level and seemingly required changes to systems and processes. This was too much to bite off and quick wins were required, as previous big change initiatives had burned the finders of management.

Employing the customer needs model and identifying needs for information, interaction, and transactions allowed the team to develop a strategy to move forward. This approach enabled the organization to meet customer needs early without requiring major changes.

Starting with information, the team engaged existing customers on the road with the sales teams and discovered that a major customers' issue was their ability to understand the contract they had and configure it to fit their needs. This provided an opportunity to address this need with an online tool that enabled customers to compile their own requirements in their own language. This gave them more clarity about the options they had and often led to their taking up more features than previously.

The team brought these new approaches to market through pilots and local work with sales centers. As they proved successful, they rolled them out to the wider organization. This proved to add to the agile approach by enabling life improvements and developments.

Throughout the work there was a concern about whether we would hit some underlying transactional issues that would slow the development of the approach. However, we discovered that a lot of what had been thought to be transactional issues went away as customers were clearer on the proposition and had better information and interactions with the firm.

Takeaway Messages

1. Have separate strategies to meet customers' information, interaction, and transaction needs.
2. Move changes forward at different speeds to realize quick wins.
3. Fixing informational needs takes the weight of the transactional side, too.

Chapter 6

Tools

Throughout this book we discuss how to use various tools to tackle business challenges. In this section we explain the most frequently used tools in more detail. For more service design tools, visit www.liveworkstudio.com/SDforB

CUSTOMER PROFILES

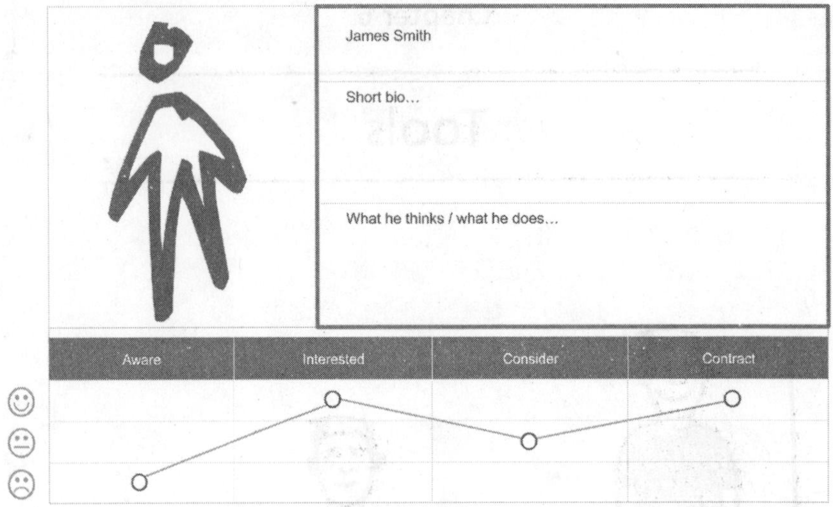

Businesses have to design their operations to deliver to thousands of customers. To do this they standardize and create processes and operations that enable efficient delivery for many customers. Much market research follows this same pattern by analyzing customers in the thousands to define a market size or put a number to a qualitative factor such as desirability. However, this focus can cause the business to lose touch with customers as human beings, who they need to be able to relate to as individuals. We also need insight into the experiences and motivations of individual people.

A core tool to counter this effect is the customer profile. A customer profile is a simple portrait of an individual customer (B2C or B2B) that brings the customers—with their specific context needs and experiences—into discussions within the business. Profiles differ from a lot of research and insight, as they do not pretend to be comprehensive; rather, they are specific to a customer and the truth of that customer's experience and needs.

Profiles are easily accessed and consumed descriptions of a customer. They are created from direct testimony from customers through an interview, conversation, or shadowing. Profiles use direct quotations from interviews, a photograph, and a description of the person's experience of the service—the ups and the downs. A profile should summarize an interview or conversation in a way that others get a feel for what the customers are like and what is important to them.

Customer profiles can be developed for business customers as well as consumers. When your customer is a business you can describe the business in terms of its situation, character, and strategic priorities. It is also important to describe a number of key actors in the business—the check signer and the end user, for example—to give a feel for the relationships that characterize the business. They should focus on the priorities of that business and help you to get a feel for how your products and services fit into their priorities and day-to-day work.

When creating a customer profile, think about the specifics of the people you met. Start with their background and context before going into how they felt about the company you represented. Think about the journey they have been on to get to where they are today and then zoom into specific experiences that they had (irritating or delightful) that give you an insight into what they value.

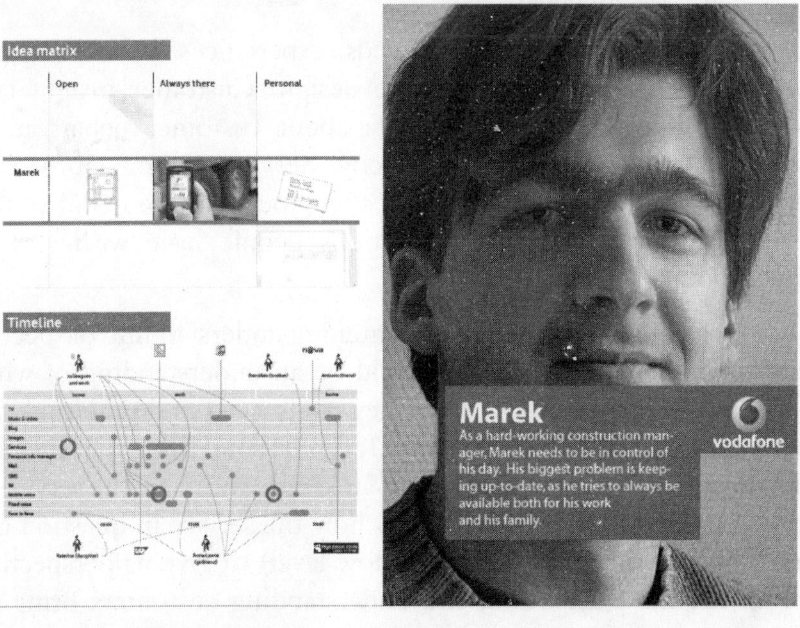

Customer Profile Example

Customer profiles enable insights into customer experience to be shared with a wider team or whole organization. They help designers to have a customer in mind when designing a service and help humanize presentations by basing them on real human beings.

CUSTOMER INSIGHTS

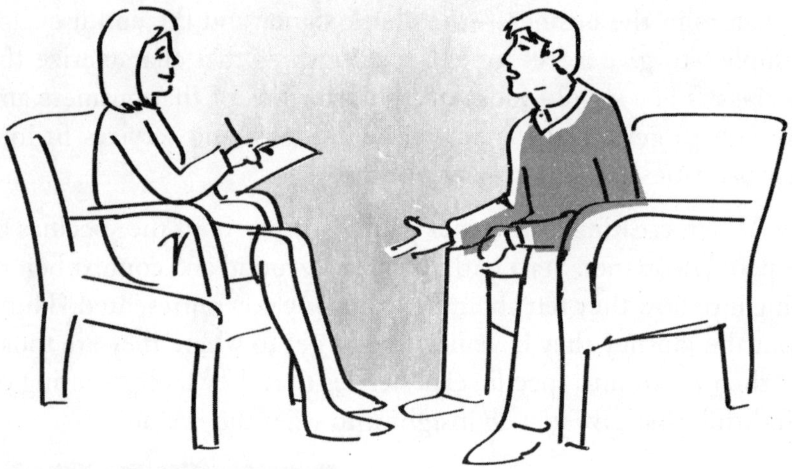

Insight into customers—their needs, experiences, behaviors, and motivations—is key to all service design. Customer insight can come from prior experience, data about customer behavior, or firsthand observation and testimony. Service design approaches differ from traditional research in their focus on the detail of the lived experience and the interactions people have with service touch-points and interfaces.

A customer insight is an enlightening understanding of specific customers' perspectives. This could be an understanding of what they find most frustrating, what they really need to do their job, or what they really don't understand. It can be something that they do but do not understand that gives us an insight into how the service is failing them. Often a key insight is how the service in question fits into their world (often at quite a low level) to give us perspective about the time, attention, and understanding customers bring to their interactions with the service. Insight is also a way to tell stories about customers in a way that cuts through all the data and gets to the human story.

An insight could come through data. We could look at complaints and see what are the majority of issues that customers have. This gives us a clear indication of where a problem lies. It may not tell us why it is a problem.

To probe this issue further we may want to observe the interaction about which the complaint is made. Why is the customer concerned about this issue, what is the level of his or her frustration? This will give a more qualitative insight into the experience and its importance. It will also enable us to see the interaction firsthand and understand the dynamics.

Some challenges cannot be investigated in such a simple form. Or we may be interested in the more longitudinal picture of a customer relationship to understand the relative ups and downs of an experience. In addition, we may be looking for a more external insight into unmet customer needs that could be the fuel for innovation. To do this it is important to engage customers more directly and discuss their experience of a particular domain. For example, if we wanted to understand opportunities to innovation in the house-buying market we would need to understand the experience people have and identify unmet needs or specific pain points they have in this process.

To do this we can shadow people at different stages of the process to create a composite picture of the whole and also debrief people who have recently undertaken a move to understand their experience. Using journey maps as stimulus for these discussions and asking people to draw it for you can help them recall the steps they took and how they felt at each point.

Finally, insights come from every customer engagement but must be compiled into a more comprehensive whole. To do this we look for repetition of themes from multiple people and correlation of qualitative insight with quantitative data.

A customer interview in progress

Customer insights drive both improvement and innovation in service design. The skill is in designing a research approach that will give you the specifics you need. For improvement you need granular detail to be able to reengineer a specific journey. For innovation you need more external understanding of the customers' world.

CUSTOMER JOURNEYS

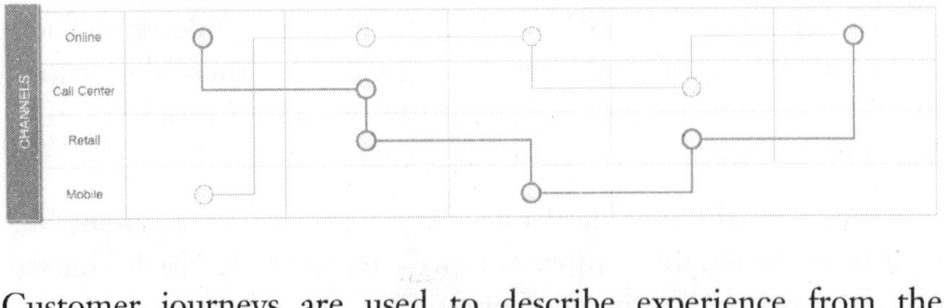

Customer journeys are used to describe experience from the customer's perspective. Unlike process mapping they look at things in terms of what customers must do and the interactions they have on the journey. Customer journeys are used to get into details on customer experiences, to understand their needs at a granular level, and to redesign journeys to enable better outcomes.

A customer journey describes the steps that customers go through when they use a service. Unlike a lifecycle, which structures the customer relationship, there can be many and different customer journeys. Customer journeys also focus on specific parts of the experience; they enable us to focus on a specific aspect of an overall experience such as an onboarding journey or a specific use of the service such as a routine visit. The analogies with actual journeys help you think of a customer journey as a train ride within a wider relationship over time with a train operator.

To develop a customer journey it is important to understand the experience from the customer perspective. A good guess can be made in many cases when there is knowledge in the team about the journey. These assumptions can then be validated through more direct shadowing or interviews with customers.

It is equally important to review a customer journey with experts who understand the processes of the case in point. There will be aspects of the journey that the customers do not see but have an influence on their experience. Processing applications or scheduling appointments are general examples.

Describe the journey in customer terms so that you are able to have a conversation with the customer about the experience without jargon. This also helps to get colleagues into a customer mind-set when they use the journey.

Once a journey is defined, a number of structural considerations can be mapped to the journey. You can map the data you have from research—qualitative in terms of customer needs and pain points or quantitative such as drop-off numbers of satisfaction scores. We can also map customer engagement to the journey in terms of the touchpoints and channels used. Armed with this data, new improvements or innovation scenarios and interactions can also be described using the journey for structure.

Dixons Online/In-store Service Blueprint: **'Researcher' Typology**

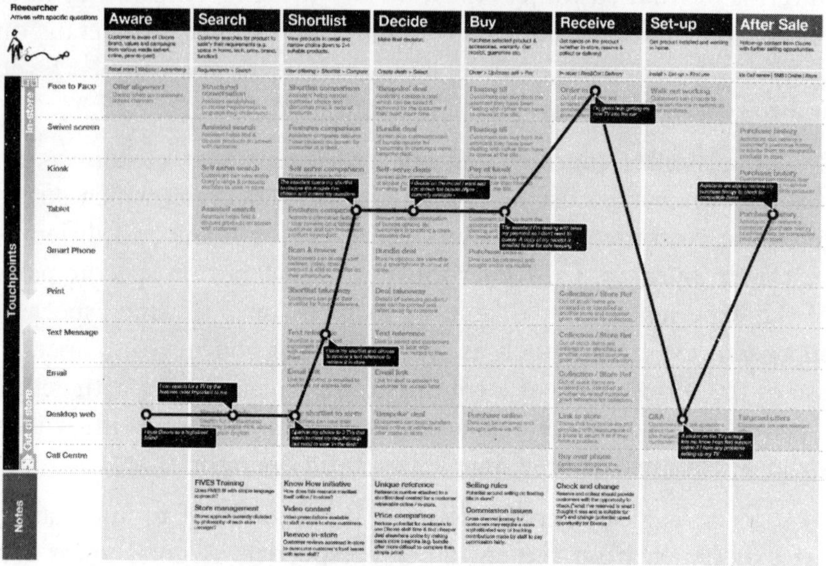

An example of a customer journey

A customer journey enables you to focus on customer experience as a movement through stages that can be understood and improved on. By using customer terms it helps bring an outside-in focus on either new scenarios or analysis of the specific issues that are preventing a journey from being as effective as possible.

CUSTOMER LIFECYCLES

A customer lifecycle is a strategic tool to understand your business and how customers fit into it. It is a framework that can be employed for a number of different analyses from understanding customer behavior trends to designing customer centricity strategies.

A customer lifecycle describes the phases and stages customers move through during their relationship with a sector. Customers who use a particular sector—say, car insurance—are somewhere in the lifecycle whether with one company or another. This cycle runs through the phases before they buy or join, the purchase or contract point, the early setup, and day-to-day during a relationship. Finally, it covers the process of reconsideration and leaving.

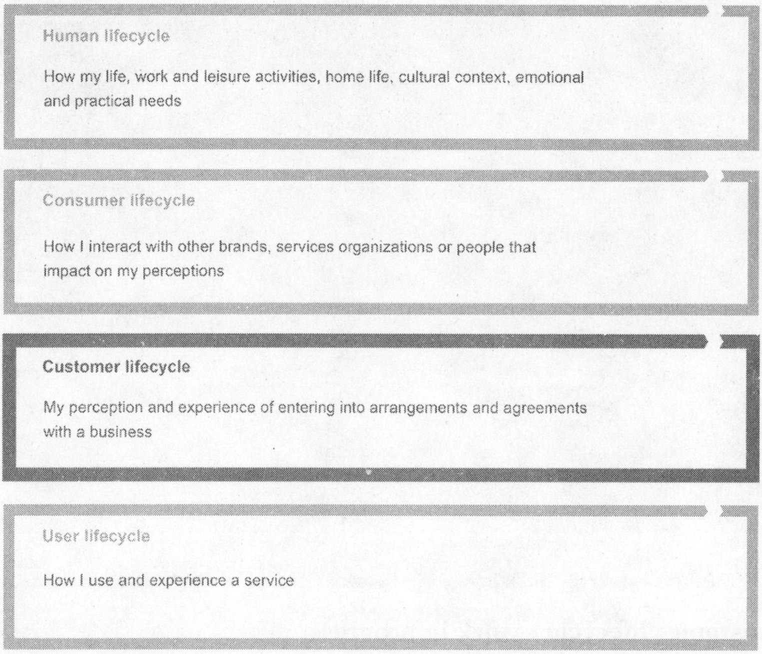

Customer lifecycles

A customer lifecycle has a specific structure or rhythm as described earlier. The four general phases of *before*, *begin*, *during*, and *after* apply to all customer relationships. Each sector will have differences in the specific phases and the language used but will have common structural elements. For example, all services should be aware of the need for customers to consider the offer, to set it up for themselves, to be able to change their usage, and to have incidents responded to.

As customer lifecycles provide a strong and shared framework for a number of different concerns in a business, it is important that they are strongly validated and communicated within the organization. Running validation workshops with experts and a cross-section of people to check that it is understood and the phases and stages are current and accepted is essential. Following this clear communication and dissemination is important.

A customer lifecycle is like a backbone for customer experience and service design work. It provides a structure that a lot of

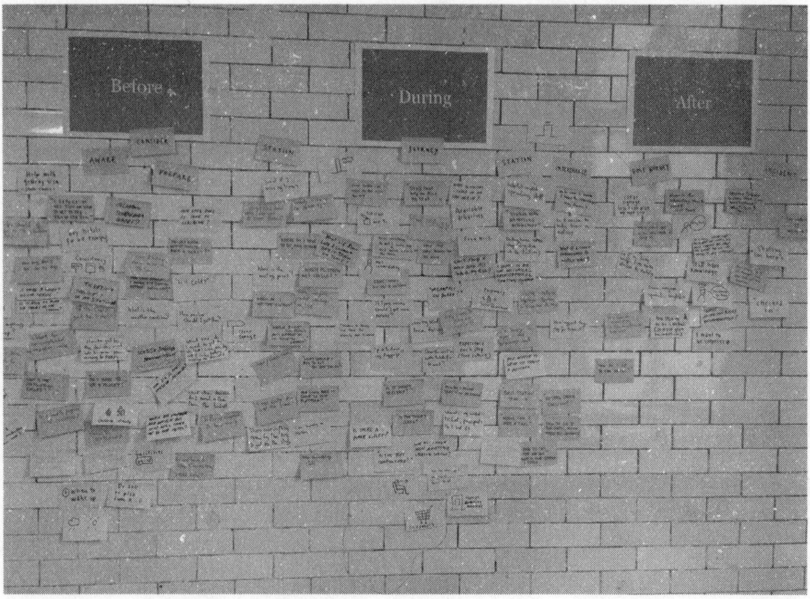

A customer lifecycle - work in progress

different work can be connected to and enables transferral of work and ultimately an accurate analysis of issues and opportunities.

CROSS-CHANNEL VIEWS

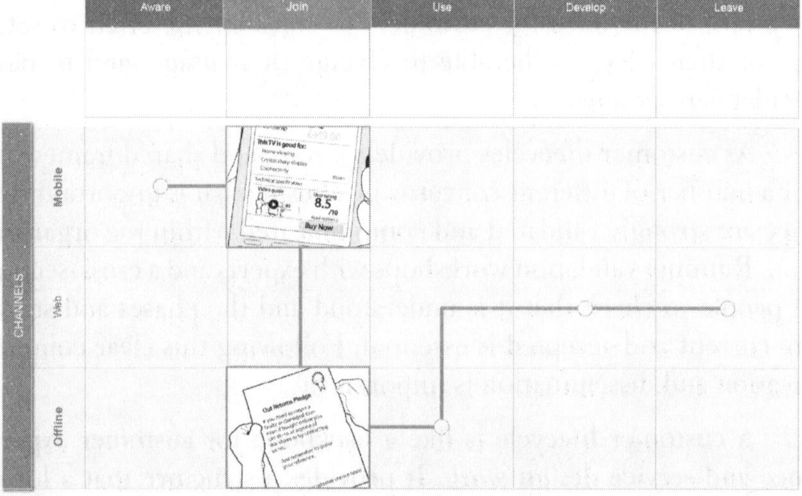

When designing services, a key consideration is how the channels come together. How do we use a range of channels in a unified way to deliver services to customers in a way that fits their needs? Additionally, how do we help customers to move from one channel to another or encourage their migration to a more effective channel? A cross-channel view used in conjunction with a customer journey is a powerful and highly visual tool for ensuring this holistic and strategic view.

A cross-channel view will map each channel as a "swim lane" in relation to a customer lifecycle or journey. This enables us to show what is happening in each channel and look at the channels in relation to one another.

The first step is to define the channels under consideration. What are the current or potential ways that you engage customers? These could be face-to-face, web, mobile, phone, and so on. Channels could also be places such as retail, clinic, classroom, and so on. Sometimes to keep it simple it is good to just have two channels: human and digital. This allows you to think about what parts of the service need a human touch and what can be codified into a digital interaction, then work out how the two work together.

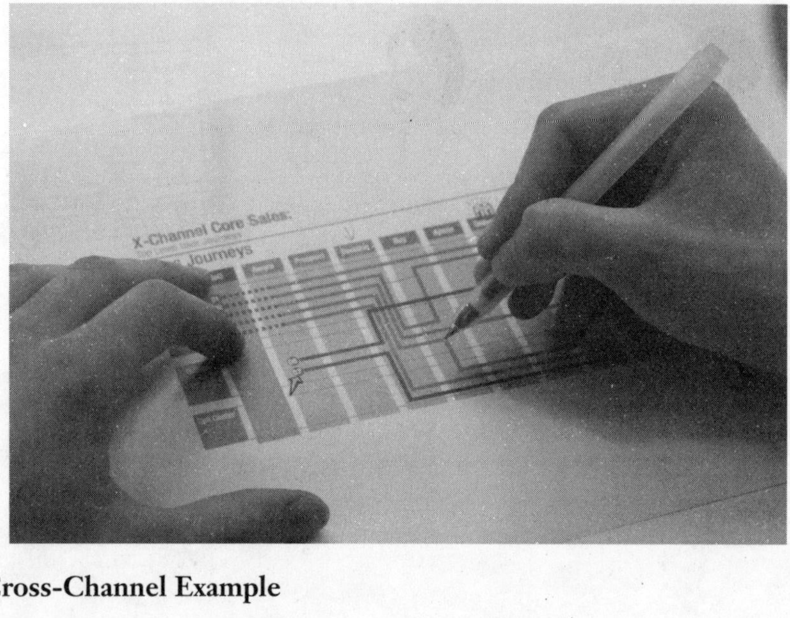

Cross-Channel Example

Channel views can be used to map the current *as is* situation or a future *to be* design or the gap between the two. *As is* is about capturing all the interactions that customers currently have. This can show the gaps between channels as customers struggle to transition. *To be* enables you to describe how you want the channels to work together in the future.

It is important to remember that different customer types have different channel needs. This may be with the customer's situation, technical awareness, or confidence, and the level of support they need in a specific task. We can map the journey that different customers have through a multichannel service by drawing a line on top of the channel map.

Cross-channel views help to manage a multichannel service. They provide a visual mapping of the channels and how they work together. Used in conjunction with customer journeys and profiles issues can be identified and strategies can be developed for better use of the channels at your disposal.

SERVICE SCENARIOS

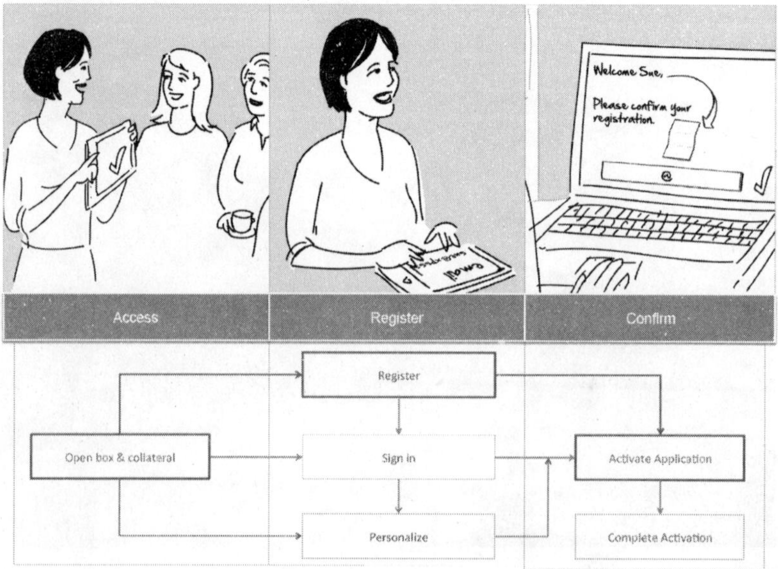

In any kind of change, be it radical innovation or incremental improvement, there is a need to understand the possible and desired future situation for the business, and most importantly, for the customer. Being clear on the options for the future and using this clarity to make decisions is a critical requirement.

Service scenarios are invaluable in developing a clear picture of future options and future targets. Scenarios focus on defining the future customer experience and how it will impact business and operations. Service scenarios provide a clear picture of future options and future targets.

Service scenarios tell the story about how customers will move through all or parts of your service. They could describe a new travel experience on a future train or dive specifically into the adoption experience of a new technology. Scenarios are like stories in that they should have a clearly defined context, characters (customers, staff, brands, etc.), and motivations. This context provides the start point for building a future story. For example, new customers in growing industries want to be able to test technologies before they

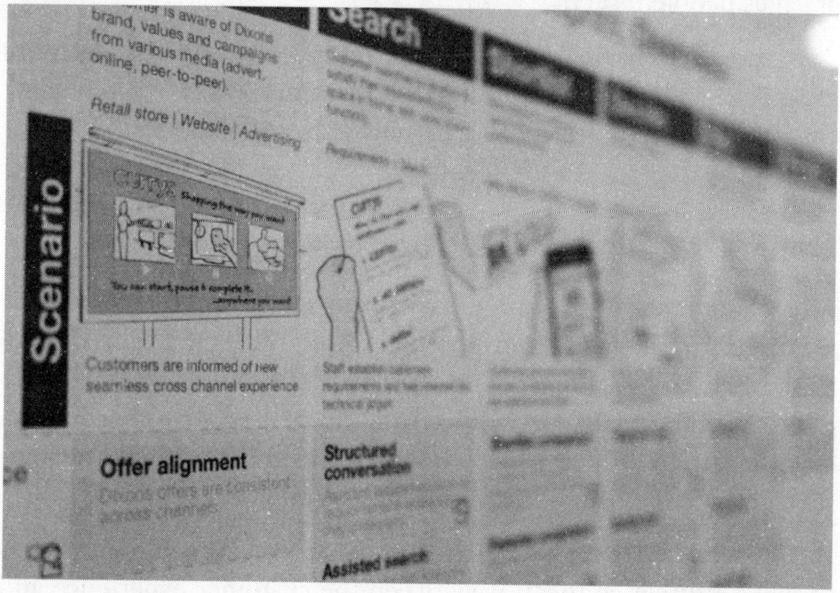

An example of a service scenario

buy them. Scenarios can then be brought to life with storytelling techniques such as narrative description, story boarding, or even video that describe how the customers' needs could be met.

Scenarios can be used to explore a range of options for a future service. They could look at how different business strategies will affect the customer experience or how different customer types could have different versions on a service (say a regular commuter versus a tourist on our new train). This use of scenarios helps to ensure services cater to different needs.

Scenarios should be seen as flexible tools that can be adapted and changed, challenged, and validated, used at all stages of a process from initial concept to final specification. It is a good idea to make them sketchy at first so they do not feel like a done deal and to develop their resolution as your plans become more concrete.

Scenarios are invaluable in engaging others in a change. They can be used to discuss your strategy with partners and senior management or engage frontline staff in options for how their jobs will change. In both cases they bring the concept to life in a way that engages people directly.

Service scenarios enable a team to explore future options more creatively, with greater customer focus and in a way that can quickly engage others in a project to gain buy-in or collaboration.

ORGANIZATIONAL IMPACT ANALYSIS

Any customer-driven change has an impact on the delivery organization. Any service design that does not understand this is going to struggle to make an impact, as it will not understand the scale of complexity of change. Connecting the desired customer experience designs to the organizational structures and capabilities enables smart choices to be made or impact to be quantified.

A service design approach to organizational impact analysis is to make a direct connection between the customer experience and the delivery mechanisms. In the same way as we can create swim

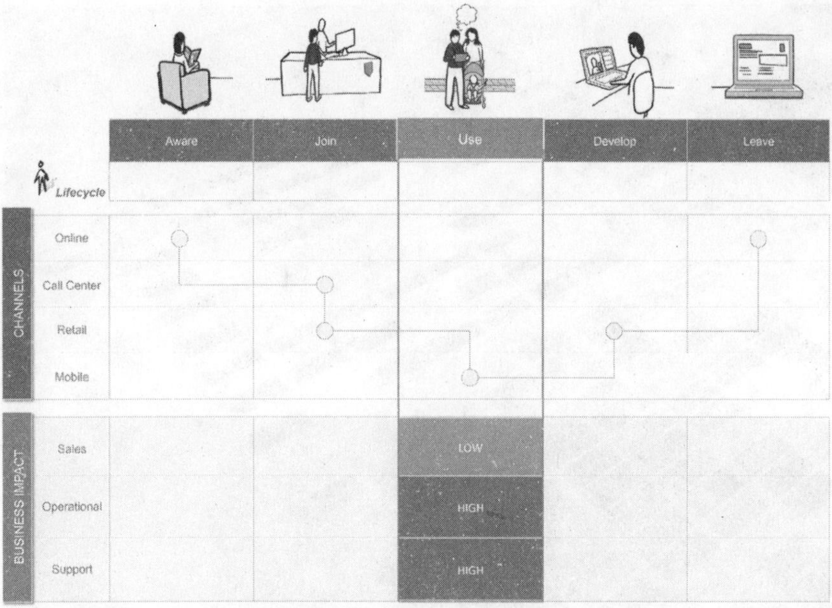

Organizational Impact Diagram

lanes to define how channels deliver a customer experience at each stage of the customer journey, we can categorize business capabilities or structures in the same way. This enables us to identify where a change for customers has an organizational impact.

Once you have defined a customer journey you can create parallel swim lanes to represent different aspects of the organization. We can use this to analyze the organizational capabilities and their qualities. For example, in relation to customers' experience of setup, the capability to onboard new customers is a mix of processes, systems, people, and policies (business rules). Using these categories we can explore two things. We can look at the maturity or strength of this capability and how well it is delivering on customer need. Using the qualities we can identify if the issues are in one specific area and what the root cause could be.

When designing a new service or improvement the same approach can be used to work with cross-functional teams to understand what needs to be developed in order to be able

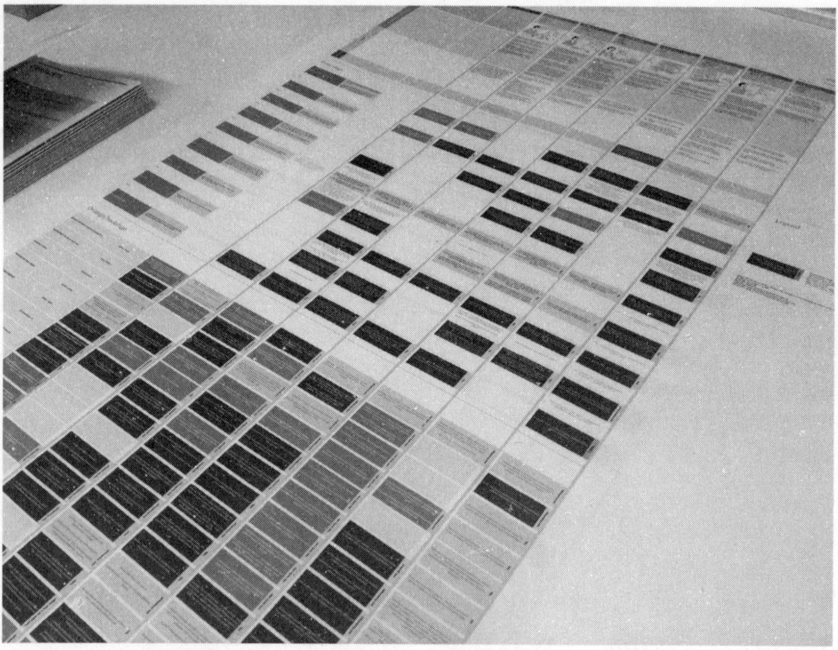

Organizational Impact Example

to deliver the new service. This work can be used to inform investment planning and road map decisions.

A related way to view the organizational impact is on functions or departments. Rather than use the qualities, we can map swim lanes for each key area of the business such as sales, marketing, operations, and customer service. This is useful if the analysis we want is more about engagement and managing change between stakeholders and staff. If we are aware early that a change will have a legal impact, we can engage the legal team early in discussions about what we are trying to achieve rather than later when they have little time of engagement.

An organizational impact analysis is an essential part of how service design moved concepts into the organization and navigated the challenges of changing the machinery of the business. It is not a one-off activity but an ongoing way to facilitate the dialogue between all the people and moving parts that contribute to a successful service delivery.

CREATIVE DESIGN WORKSHOPS

Workshops are a widely used tool for bringing together people to work together on a task. Service design has its own style of workshop that is both collaborative and creative. We use workshops at all phases of work and use visual tools and templates to enable participants to be more structured and creative in the work they do. These templates also enable higher quality capture of the thoughts and ideas that emerge through the workshops. A workshop is about getting from a to b in a process, achieving a specific task. For illustration here are four workshop types for differed stages of a project.

Understand

The goal of an understand workshop is to create a shared definition of a problem or opportunity. The workshop approach is to focus on customers or service users and capture what is known about their experiences and needs. Understand workshops can be used to explore either the opportunity for innovation or improvement work. For innovation the goal is to uncover unmet needs in a customer group as the source for new opportunities. For improvement the focus is on the current experience of a businesses' customer base to identify priority areas for intervention.

Imagine

Imagine workshops bring teams together to build service scenarios based on a shared understanding of customers. These are creative sessions where the goal is to develop concepts for service innovation or improvement. Our workshops use visualization and storytelling to bring ideas to life.

Imagine workshops vary from large events designed to gather ideas from a diverse group to focused sessions with a core team to build concepts together. The common thread is that concepts are built on both customer insight and business goals, and those ideas are evaluated based on clear objectives and scope.

Design

Design workshops are used to move a project from concept toward a detailed view of the customer experience. A typical workshop would take a scenario and develop ideas for the delivery of that experience. Using service-blueprinting techniques, we can build a picture of the experience across channels working with multiple functions of an organization to ensure a shared view.

Design workshops are used to develop both front-stage (customer experience) and back-stage (business requirements) aspects of a service. They have huge value in bringing together different responsibilities across an organization or different suppliers to ensure a consistent view and clear shared understanding.

Create

Create workshops provide customer experience governance on go-to-market or service upgrade projects. Projects with multiple connected work streams benefit from guided sessions to align

A workshop in progress

deliverables and check that the customer experience and business goals are being upheld. Often adaptations are required to negotiate barriers encountered during the project, and a multidisciplinary team can develop the best solutions.

Create workshops deliver clearly understood updates to service designs and enable those responsible for business enablers such as IT or process design to ensure that their work is in line with strategic requirements and customer experience ambitions.

Acknowledgements

We would like to thank the following people who have been essential to the development of this book. The Livework team, past and present, whose work and creativity has provided us with the ability to grow and develop our business and practice and whose projects provide the material for this book. Livework clients (also past and present) who have provided us with the challenges and feedback that has helped us write a book for business. Our families who put up with the late nights writing. The Wiley team for accommodating our foibles. Melissa for the amazing illustrations. Mark for saying 'how high?' when we asked him to jump. And finally, but most importantly, Wendy without whose amazing editing the book would be far less readable.

INDEX

Note: Page references in *italics* refer to figures.